Endor

If you are looking for a guide to make the Letters of John fresh and interesting again, this is the book for you! There are parallels between John and the Qumran literature and the Mishnah. For example, through a consideration of the Jewish sources you may find new insights into the spiritual meaning of water and cleansing used by John.

—Dr. William D. (Bill) Bjoraker, Associate Professor of Judeo-Christian Studies and Contemporary Western Culture, William Carey International University, Pasadena, Cal.

While engaging with traditional and well-established New Testament commentators, Brumbach raises a key set of issues and questions that has largely been eclipsed by the parting of the ways between Judaism and Christianity.

—Dr. Jennifer M. Rosner, Affiliate Assistant Professor of Systematic Theology at Fuller Theological Seminary, Pasadena, Cal.

I recommend this work for all who are interested in being gently initiated into an up-to-date, concise, yet comprehensive treatment of John's letters.

—Joseph Shulam, Director of Netivyah Bible Instruction Ministry, Jerusalem, Israel

This accessible yet scholarly commentary does readers the needed service of moving the Johannine Letters out of the realm of anti-Jewish polemic and into the realm of intra-Jewish dialogue. Rabbi Brumbach carefully highlights how the letters reveal a community wrestling with what it means to love one another for the sake of HaShem (the Name)', especially when there are divisions and defections. There is life-giving word here for all current believers.

—Dr. Nicholas J. Zola, Associate Professor of Religion, Pepperdine University, Malibu, Cal.

Rabbi Brumbach interacts with the text of the letters and with current scholarship to explain John's messages in terms of Late Second Temple Jewish life and thought. An excellent brief commentary on John's letters!

—Rabbi Dr. Carl Kinbar, Director, New School for Jewish Studies

A MESSIANIC COMMENTARY

JOHN'S THREE LETTERS

ON
HOPE, LOVE AND COVENANT FIDELITY

A MESSIANIC COMMENTARY

John's
Three Letters

ON
Hope, Love and Covenant Fidelity

Rabbi Joshua Brumbach

Lederer Books
An imprint of
Messianic Jewish Publishers
Clarksville, MD 21029

1   2019

ISBN 978-1-73393-545-6

Library of Congress Control Number:2019944016

Published by
Lederer Books
An imprint of
Messianic Jewish Publishers
6120 Day Long Lane
Clarksville, Maryland 21029

Distributed by
Messianic Jewish Resources Int'l.
www.messianicjewish.net
Individual and Trade Order line: 800-410-7647

Email: lederer@messianicjewish.net

Printed in the United States of America

ACKNOWLEDGMENTS

עֲשֵׂה לְךָ רַב וּקְנֵה לְךָ חָבֵר

Get yourself a teacher and acquire yourself a friend.

Pirkei Avot 1.6

For my teachers and mentors, including:
Rabbi Murray Silberling
Pastors Mike and Nancy Prato
Rabbi Warren and Rabbanit Shirel Dean
Rabbi David and Sandy Levine
Dr. David and Martha Stern
And the many colleagues whom
I have learned both with and from.

I am incredibly grateful for my wife, Monique, who has always been my greatest support and closest friend. I am also thankful for our son, Gilad, who sacrificed playtime with Abba while I worked on this book. And to my parents and family, your love and support is always appreciated.

Additional acknowledgements are also necessary for those who provided useful challenges and feedback, especially Dr. Nick Zola. I would also like to express my appreciation to our congregation, Beth Emunah, for their role in this project. The framework for this commentary began as a series of sermons through John's Letters. Specific feedback and encouragement from various individuals was helpful as I continued working on the manuscript for this book.

I would also like to thank the publisher, Rabbi Barry Rubin, and those at Lederer/Messianic Jewish Publishers.

Finally, I would also like to express my deepest respect and appreciation for Dr. David and Martha Stern and for their regular encouragement to me personally, and to our family. Unless otherwise noted, all biblical citations are from the *Complete Jewish Bible* (Clarksville: Jewish New Testament Publications, 1998), with minor alterations based on my own discretion to emphasize the underlying Greek, highlight a particular idea, or clarify the English translation.

CONTENTS

GENERAL EDITOR'S PREFACE

Nearly all bible commentators emphasize the importance of understanding the historical, cultural and grammatical aspects of any text of scripture. As has been said, "A text without a context is a pretext." In other words, to assume one can understand what God has revealed through those who present his word—prophets, poets, visionaries, apostles— without knowing the context is presumption. To really understand God's word, it's essential to know something about who wrote it and to whom, what was actually said and what it originally meant, when, where, and why it was written.

By now, everyone knows that the New Testament is a thoroughly Jewish book, written nearly entirely by Jews, taking place in and around Israel. The people written about—Paul, Peter, James, John, etc.—were almost all Jews who never abandoned their identities or people. The topics covered—sin, salvation, resurrection, Torah, Sabbath, how to "walk with God," the Millennium, etc.—were all Jewish topics that came from the Hebrew scripture. The expressions used often were Jewish idioms of that day. So, to fully understand the New Testament, it must be viewed through "Jewish eyes," meaning that the Jewish historical, cultural, grammatical must be examined.

There are commentaries for women, for men, for teens, even for children. There are commentaries that focus on financial issues in the bible. Others provide archaeological material. Some commentaries are topical. Others are the works of eminent men and women of God. But, until now, no commentary series has closely looked at the Jewish context of the New Testament books.

In this series, we have invited some of the top Messianic Jewish theologians in the world to contribute their knowledge and understanding. Each has written on a book (or more) of the New Testament they've specialized in, making sure to present the Jewish aspects—the original context—of each book. These works are not meant to be a verse-by-verse exegetical commentary. There are already many excellent ones available. But, these commentaries supplement what others lack, by virtue of the fact they focus on the Jewish aspects.

A number of different authors wrote these commentaries, each in his own style. Just as the Gospels were written by four different men, each with his own perspective and style, these volumes, too, have variations. We didn't want the writers to have to conform too much to any particular style guide, other than our basic one.

You may see some Hebrew expressions or Hebrew transliterations of the names in the New Testament. Thus, one writer might refer to the Apostle to the Gentiles as Paul. Another might write, Shaul, Paul's Hebrew name. Still, another might write Saul, an Anglicized version of Shaul. And some might write Saul/Paul, to reflect, not reject the different ways this servant of Messiah was known.

Another variation is the amount of reference material. Some have ample footnotes or endnotes, while others incorporate references within the text. Some don't have an enormous amount of notes, based on the book they are writing commentary for.

We have plans for a Messianic Jewish commentary series on the entire bible. Although much has been written on the books of the Hebrew Scriptures, and there have been some written by Messianic Jews, there hasn't been a full commentary series on the "Older" Testament. But, we hope to publish such a series in the near future.

So, I invite you to put on your Jewish glasses (if you're not Jewish) and take a look at the New Testament in a way that will truly open up new understanding for you, as you get to know the God of Israel and his Messiah better.

RABBI BARRY RUBIN
General Editor and Publisher

AUTHOR'S PREFACE

John's Three Letters include some of the most beloved and often-quoted portions of scripture. Countless sermons have been given on their verses, and they are intimately familiar to innumerable individuals across time. Therefore, most people conversant on the Bible – scholars included – are confident they already have John's letters figured out.

But have they really?

There is a need for a fresh and post-supersessionist reading of John's letters that challenges common presuppositions regarding their purpose, message and relevance. By delving into their original Jewish context we will discover a world of hope, love, and God's ongoing covenant-faithfulness to Israel. We will also demonstrate that the author's theology, particularly his understanding of the divine nature of Messiah, was thoroughly embedded within the Jewish world of the first century.

This work is not intended to be an overly technical commentary on every detail, theory, word, or verse in relation to the study of John or his letters. There are already a number of great commentaries that do so.[1] Instead, the purpose of this volume is to provide a broad exploration of these epistles, focusing on the thoroughly Jewish context, message, and overall purpose of John's letters, drawing on the cutting edge of biblical scholarship while presenting the material in an accessible, contemporary, and spiritually meaningful way.

We will explore these letters in three parts. The first section is a general contextual introduction that will provide a basic framework for understanding the second part, which is a running commentary on each epistle. Each book contains a short introduction followed by its commentary. To make it easier to follow along and reference, I have quoted each letter in its entirety, commenting on particular verses and passages. Reflection questions have also been included at the end of each chapter for individual and small group studies.

In the Conclusion we will discuss the relevance of John's letters for today and their personal application for spiritual life. Finally, a helpful glossary has also been included for certain words, references, concepts, and persons the reader might not already be familiar with.

---

1. For more in-depth, technical commentaries see: Karen H. Jobes, *1, 2, & 3 John* (Zondervan Exegetical Commentary on the New Testament, 19, Grand Rapids: Zondervan, 2014); Colin G. Kruse, *The Letters of John* (The Pillar New Testament Commentary, Grand Rapids: Eerdmans, 2000); Robert Y. Yarbrough, *1-3 John* (Baker Exegetical Commentary on the New Testament, Grand Rapids: Baker Academic, 2008); among others.

INTRODUCTION

The Letters of John offer us a window into the earliest circles of Yeshua-followers,[1] when the apostles were still influential leaders and the movement's adherents were still primarily Jewish (although this was rapidly changing). They were written during a tumultuous time and reveal some of the issues and concerns these earliest followers wrestled with. John's letters are also interrelated with his Gospel and expose a specific "time of dispute between believers involving both theological and behavioral concerns."[2] The author seeks to correct these distortions and provide encouragement and important lessons in faith.

State of Johannine Studies

Before we proceed it is important to provide a brief summary of Johannine scholarship, as well as some important developments relevant to our study of John's Letters. This will help the reader

---

1. The earliest followers of Jesus knew him by his original Hebrew name, Yeshua (ישוע), the masculine form of the word for Salvation/Redemption, ישועה). Although not commonly used in academic works, in an attempt to more accurately portray the historical Jesus, and to specifically emphasize the Jewish context out of which he emerged, the name Yeshua will primarily be used except when quoting others.
2. Colin G. Kruse, *The Letters of John* (The Pillar New Testament Commentary, Grand Rapids: Eerdmans, 2000), 1.

grasp how this work contributes to, and also differs, from previous assumptions within Johannine studies. One of the dominant thrusts until very recently has been to understand John's gospel (and letters) not as the product of a single author, but a compilation and redaction of a community – the Johannine community. According to Karen H. Jobes:

> The dominant approach to Johannine studies for the last few decades perceived difficulties with John's gospel that were thought to be solved by an elaborate reconstruction of its redactional history with one or more corresponding historical scenarios involving the Johannine community. Scholars ... dominated the field in the second half of the twentieth century with their theories for the composition of John's gospel and letters that focused on the conjectured issues of the late first-century Johannine community, supposedly expelled from the Jewish synagogues, than on [an accurate account of] the life and teachings of Jesus.[3]

Richard Baukham, in his work *The Testimony of the Beloved Disciple*[4] provides a helpful summary of other prevailing assumptions (which I have further summarized below):

1. The Beloved Disciple (in the Fourth Gospel) is neither John the son of Zebedee nor the author of the Gospel.

2. As an account of history, the Gospel of John is far less reliable than the Synoptics because it is primarily a work of theology rather than history.

---

3. Karen H. Jobes, *1, 2, & 3 John* (Zondervan Exegetical Commentary on the New Testament, 19, Grand Rapids: Zondervan, 2014), 13.
4. Richard Bauckham, *The Testimony of the Beloved Disciple* (Grand Rapids: Baker Academic, 2007), 10-12.

3. The Gospel of John is the product of a complex history of literary composition which has left the marks of its various stages on the text as we have it, making it possible to reconstruct its literary prehistory.

4. The Gospel is the product of and written for the so-called Johannine community, a small and idiosyncratic branch of early believers, sectarian in character, isolated from the rest of the early movement, and formed by its own particular history and conflicts.

5. A "two-level" reading of the Fourth Gospel narrative assumes that the Gospel's story of Yeshua is also to be understood as the story of the Johannine community. Therefore, the various stages of the composition of the Gospel are held to reflect developments in the history of the Johannine community. The reconstructed history of the text and the reconstructed history of the community are inseparable.

6. There is broad agreement that this history focuses on the Johannine community's relationship to the wider Jewish matrix in which it arose and from which it later painfully separated. Therefore, the Gospel [and letters] provide an increasingly bitter and polemical attitude to the parent body from which it had separated.

To summarize even further ... there is no single author, the Fourth Gospel is a complex creation of a later community inspired by the teachings of an original apostle who developed a theological narrative of Yeshua (rather than a historical one), and that hidden within that account is also an intentional creative narrative of the community that produced it.

However, these assumptions have also been challenged in recent years. A growing voice of scholars now argue that we should not rule out the possibility of a single author, and that the Johannine writings do provide a reliable and historic portrayal of Yeshua's life and teachings. There is also pushback against the long-held "speculative reconstructions of the Johannine community" which were assumptions of an extensive redactional history.[5] Furthermore, there has also been a growing appeal to read and interpret these writings from within their original Jewish contextual framework and from a non-supersessionist point of view.

Which John?

It has been traditionally taught that the Epistles and the Fourth Gospel were authored by John (יוחנן - *Yochanan* in Hebrew and Ἰωάννης - *Iōannēs* in Greek). However, which "John" is this referring to, as this was a very popular and common Jewish name.

The earliest traditions ascribe authorship to the apostle John the son of Zebedee, who was one of Yeshua's chosen twelve.[6] The first recorded support for the apostle John's authorship comes from Polycarp, the bishop of Smyrna (d. 156), who was a disciple of John; and from Papias, a contemporary of Polycarp, whose writings survive only as quotations in the later writings of Irenaeus and Eusebius.

According to Jobes:

> Polycarp and Papias lived in the greater vicinity of Ephesus in western Asia Minor, the location to which the apostle John is said to have fled at about the time when the Romans destroyed the temple in Jerusalem (AD 70), taking Mary the mother of

---

5. Jobes, *op. cit.,* 14.
6. Ibid., 22.

Jesus with him. There he presumably lived for the rest of his long life … Irenaeus (175-195), bishop of Lyon, was born in Asia Minor and as a child personally knew Polycarp, who is said to have been appointed bishop of Smyrna by eyewitnesses of the Lord Jesus. Irenaeus says that John, the disciple of the Lord who was with Jesus in the upper room, wrote the gospel while living in Ephesus.[7]

Other early attestations to the Apostle John's authorship come from Tertullian (d. after ca. 220) and from Dionysius of Alexandria (d. ca. 265).[8]

But not all scholars agree with this traditional attribution. Some agree on a single author, but argue that early references actually describe two different individuals named John. Richard Bauckham, for example, contends for "John the Elder," who although not one of the Twelve, was a Jerusalem disciple and a direct eyewitness to Yeshua. According to Bauckham, "John the Elder, to whom Papias refers to in the famous fragment of his prologue … was both the beloved disciple and the author of the Fourth Gospel (as well as the Johannine letters)."[9] He contends, "It was doubtless inevitable that this relatively unknown John should come to be identified with the famous John the son of Zebedee."[10]

Bauckham's argument, and that of other scholars who hold the position of a different Jerusalem-based disciple also named John is indeed compelling, and worth continued exploration. If true, it could help explain certain differences with the other gospel accounts.

---

7. Jobes, *op. cit.,* 22.
8. Kruse, *op. cit.,* 11.
9. Bauckham, *op. cit.,* 34. Parentheses his.
10. Ibid., 15.

However, other scholars reconcile both of these historic attestations into the same figure. Jobes argues for reading both "Johns" as referring to the same apostle:

> The witness of Papias is more complicated and has been the subject of more debate, for his writings are preserved only in those of Eusebius, whose interpretation of Papias's words raised the possibility of two men named John, one authoring the gospel and another, the elder John, the letters and the book of Revelation ... Papias mentions John twice, once as a "disciple of the Lord" and again as an "elder." But Eusebius overlooked the fact that even when Papias refers to Peter and James, he doesn't at first call them "apostles" but "elders," suggesting that the two titles were not mutually exclusive to Papias.[11]

Due to this confusion, Jobes writes, "Ever since the fourth century when Eusebius wrote, there has been debate in the church as to the authorship of the three letters attributed in the [New Testament] and about who is buried in 'John's tomb" in Ephesus."[12]

Whether Papias was referring to two different Johns or not, as Colin G. Kruse asserts, "What is clear ... is that early Christian tradition is unanimous in ascribing 1 John to John, the disciple and apostle of the Lord."[13] Furthermore, given the clear relationship in style, content and language between 1 and 2 John, and between 2 and 3 John, we can confidently propose from the textual evidence itself a single author for all three epistles.[14]

The earliest traditions of authorship, especially the witness of Polycarp, who was himself a direct disciple of John, and a reasoned assumption based on the evidence, provide plausible reasons to

11. Jobes, *op. cit.,* 22
12. Ibid., 22-23.
13. Kruse, *op. cit.,* 14.
14. Jobes, *op. cit.,* 28.

maintain a traditional view that John the son of Zebedee was the Beloved Disciple and that he (or someone close to him) authored the Fourth Gospel and the Johannine letters. According to Robert W. Yarbrough (quoting D.A. Carson), "In line with the majority view among Christian students during the past two thousand years (though out of step with today's majority), I think it highly probable that John wrote the Fourth Gospel and the three letters that traditionally bear his name."[15]

According to the Gospels, John the son of Zebedee *(Yochanan ben Zavdai)*, along with his brother, James *(Ya'akov)*, were Jewish fishermen from the Galilee. Yeshua called them to be part of his closest circle of disciples ("the Twelve") while they were out fishing one day with their father.[16]

John developed a very close relationship with Yeshua. According to the Fourth Gospel (21:20) he was the one whom Yeshua "especially loved" and who reclined against (or was seated next to) him during the final *Seder*[17] they had together. During the crucifixion it was also John whom Yeshua entrusted with the care of his mother:

> Nearby Yeshua's cross stood his mother, his mother's sister Miryam the wife of K'lofah, and Miryam from Magdala. When Yeshua saw his mother and the *talmid* whom he loved standing there, he said to his mother, "Mother, this is your son." Then he said to the *talmid*, "This is your mother." And from that time on, the *talmid* took her into his own home (John 19:25-27).

---

15. Robert W. Yarbrough, *1-3 John* (Baker Exegetical Commentary on the New Testament, Grand Rapids: Baker Academic, 2008), 5.

16. Matthew 4:21-22; Mark 1:19-20 and Luke 5:10.

17. More commonly referred to as the "Last Supper." A Seder is a special ceremonial meal for Passover. Some argue this was not a Seder, but a "pre-Passover" meal. However, even if so, it was clearly a Seder-type meal.

Following Yeshua's death and ascension, John became one of the "Three Pillars" within the leadership of the Jerusalem community. Eusebius, quoting a lost work of Clement of Alexandria writes, "Though honored as first by the Master, Peter and James and John did not contend for glory after the Savior's ascension but made James the Just bishop of Jerusalem."[18]

According to D.T. Lancaster, James the Righteous, Simon Peter, and John the son of Zebedee formed a triumvirate – a high court of three (or a *Beit Din*).[19] Paul refers to them in Galatians 2:9 as the acknowledged pillars of the assembly of Messiah. Lancaster contends[20] that each of the three had a specific role. James represented the family of Yeshua. Simon Peter ranked as first among the Twelve, and head over the Messiah's school of disciples.[21] John the son of Zebedee, the beloved disciple and an adopted son of Yeshua's mother, Mary (Miryam), stood in the unique position of representing the interests of both the family of Yeshua and his disciples. As the *nasi*[22] over the Jerusalem Council,[23] James occupied the highest position within the triumvirate.

Clement of Alexandria reports a tradition that it was the Messiah himself who singled out the three pillars: "After the resurrection, the Master imparted knowledge to James the Righteous and to

---

18. Eusebius, *Ecclesiastical History* 2.1.3 quoting Clement (Grand Rapids: Baker, 1976), 49.
19. D. Thomas Lancaster, *Holy Epistle to the Galatians* (Marshfield: First Fruits of Zion, 2011), 75-76.
20. D. Thomas Lancaster, *Torah Club: Chronicles of the Messiah,* Vol. 6 (Marshfield: First Fruits of Zion, 2011), 168.
21. Matthew 10:2; 16:17-18.
22. The term "*nasi*" is used regularly throughout the Hebrew Bible and often translated as "prince" or "captain." During the Second Temple period the term was also used for the highest ranking member of the Sanhedrin (the great assembly of sages).
23. The Council of Jerusalem was an early guiding body convened around 50/51 C.E. made up of the Apostles (Emissaries), Elders, and other prominent figures within the Yeshua-believing community. For additional information see "Jerusalem Council" in the Glossary.

John and Peter, and they imparted it to the rest of the [twelve] apostles, the rest of the apostles to the seventy."[24]

According to another early tradition, around the time Jerusalem was overtaken by the Romans and the Temple destroyed (around 70 C.E.[25]), John fled with Miryam, Yeshua's mother, to Ephesus where he composed his Gospel and Letters, and where he lived out the rest of his life. It is taught he outlived the remaining apostles and was the only one to die of natural causes, rather than a martyr's death. He died around 100 C.E. and was presumably buried in Ephesus.

Relationship of the Letters to the Gospel

It is clear that we cannot properly understand the Letters of John without referencing John's Gospel, as it visibly serves as the foundation and interpretive framework for the metaphors, images, and theology common to both.[26] As Colin G. Kruse notes, "there is a very close relationship between the Fourth Gospel and the three letters of John."[27]

Jobes also confirms, "Despite some differences that can probably be accounted for by their different genres, the letters of John and the gospel of John are closer in language, style, dualistic worldview, and theology than they are to any other [New Testament] books."[28]

Due to this close relationship, much of our discussion of the Letters will include references to John's Gospel. As Jobes explains,

---

24. Eusebius, *op. cit.,* 2.1.4 quoting Clement.
25. The abbreviations B.C.E. and C.E., which mean "Before the Common Era" and "Common Era," are commonly used among scholars instead of the more familiar B.C. ("Before Christ") and A.D. (*"Anno Domini"* which is Latin for "in the year of our Lord").
26. Jobes, *op. cit.,* 14.
27. Kruse, *op. cit.,* 2.
28. Jobes, *op. cit.,* 27.

"Because the letters of John cannot be interpreted independently of the Fourth Gospel, the currents of Johannine scholarship have largely directed interpretation of the letters as well."[29]

Relationship Between the Letters

Just as there is a clear relationship between the Fourth Gospel and the Letters, there is also a clear relationship between the letters themselves. According to Jobes:

> The themes, style, and vocabulary are so similar between 1 John and 2 John that it is hard to imagine they didn't come from the same hand. And the similarities between 2 John and 3 John – both being from "the elder," whose main concern was when to extend … hospitality (3 John) and when not to (2 John) – join them as two sides of the same coin."[30]

However, despite the clear relationship, there are a number of theories and questions as to the original order of these letters when they were written. Some scholars believe 1 John originated independently and later than 2 and 3 John. Others argue they were written by the same person at the same time and delivered together as a single package. The most common view (and the one held in this work) is that all three were written by "the elder" and probably in the same order in which they now appear in the New Testament.

It is also likely, as Jobes contends, that 1 John was written and preached by the elder within his own community during the initial schism (see more below in the section on General Purpose). But since those who broke away started spreading their false teachings

---

29. Ibid., 13.
30. Ibid., 28.

in surrounding communities as well, 2 and 3 John were letters sent out to provide correction and guidance.[31]

When Were the Letters Written?

There is general agreement that John spent his later years in and around Ephesus, and that he likely composed his gospel and letters in that city. Yarbrough confirms, "It seems warranted to think of them as reflecting conditions in the region of Ephesus in the closing decades of the first century."[32]

It is also generally accepted that the three epistles of John were written sometime in the 90's. The assumption is that if the Fourth gospel was written between 80-90 C.E., and was already widely circulated by the time the letters were written, then the epistles were likely composed between 90-95 C.E.[33] However, some scholars argue for an earlier date (some even argue for a date before the Fourth gospel). David L. Allen, for example, contends for a date between 80-85.[34] Others argue for later, between 100-110.[35]

Who Were the Intended Recipients?

John's gospel and letters were initially written to an audience within the same geographical area, in and around Ephesus in the Roman province of Asia (what we now know as the western region of Turkey). In 3 John, for example, the individuals mentioned were clearly familiar to each other, which suggests a network of congregations and communities in the same region with frequent contact.

---

31. Ibid., 29.
32. Yarbrough, *op. cit.,* 17.
33. Jobes, *op. cit.,* 29.
34. David L. Allen, *1-3 John* (Preaching the Word commentary series, Wheaton: Crossway, 2013), 19.
35. Michele Murray, "The First Letter of John," *The Jewish Annotated New Testament*, Ed. Amy-Jill Levine and Marc Zvi Brettler (New York: Oxford, 2011), 448.

These communities, like others throughout the diaspora, were originally Jewishly oriented, but often with a predominantly Gentile make-up. According to Mark D. Nanos:

> There are many indications that Christianity did develop in the context of Judaism, including synagogue attendance and the concomitant behavioral and practical ramifications that would have applied ... [W]e have good reason to believe that they would have had no concept of their faith outside the expression of the Jewish community, initially at least, for they saw their faith in continuity with the tradition of Israel's faith, that is, as the fulfillment of the promised "ingathering of the nations" that was to follow the "restoration of Israel" in Christ (Rom. 11:25-27; Acts 15:13-21).[36]

Furthermore, the size of each congregation's Jewish membership depended largely upon the demographics of the local Jewish population. By the time of Yeshua, the majority of Jews already lived outside of Israel, much like today.[37] So it was not unusual to have such communities scattered throughout the Roman Empire. Although Judea and its environs served as the Jewish homeland, and Jerusalem its holy center, the majority of the population lived scattered around the Mediterranean and in Mesopotamia, with a continually growing presence and expansion into Europe.

This became even truer following the war (Great Jewish Revolt) which resulted in the Second Temple's destruction (70 C.E.) and the expulsion of Jews from Jerusalem and its environs into the surrounding regions.

These Jewish communities located in predominantly Gentile environments faced challenges quite different from their

---

36. Mark D. Nanos, *The Mystery of Romans* (Minneapolis: Fortress Press, 1996), 71-72.
37. James 1:1 and 1 Peter 1:1.

counterparts in Israel. As a minority, Jews were always considered "other." Their strange clothing, kosher diets, worldview, monotheism, and strict moral code set them apart from those around them, and there were extreme pressures to assimilate and conform to the pagan world around them. Politically, Jews were mostly excluded from Roman citizenship, and forced to pay a unique tax, the *Fiscus Iudaicus*, due to their refusal to participate in the Imperial cult.[38]

But as Jews settled in various cities and towns across the Roman Empire they established communities that also attracted many Gentiles.[39] Ephesus was no different. Over time, these Gentiles represented a broad spectrum of affiliation. Some became full proselytes while others were God-fearers,[40] a technical category referring to Gentiles who took on various Jewish customs and observances but without fully converting to Judaism. God-fearers are regularly mentioned throughout the New Testament.[41]

F.F. Bruce, in summarizing the first-century God-fearer phenomenon, writes:

> Many Gentiles of those days, while not prepared to become full converts to Judaism (the requirement of circumcision being a special stumbling block for men), were attracted by the simple monotheism of Jewish synagogue worship and by the ethical standards of the Jewish way of life. Some of them attended synagogue and became tolerably conversant with the prayers and scripture lessons, which they heard read in the

---

38. The Imperial cult identified Roman emperors as divinely sanctioned authorities, and along with its various expected rituals, was inseparable from the worship of Rome's official deities. Jews, and later Christians, found this idea offensive refused to participate in the veneration.
39. Acts 15:20-21; et al.
40. In Greek: φοβούμενος τὸν Θεόν - *Phoboumenos ton Theon*.
41. Refer to the glossary for more on God-fearers and specific citations in the New Testament.

13

Greek version; some observed with more or less scrupulosity such distinctive Jewish practices as Sabbath observance and abstention from certain kinds of food (notably pork).[42]

As many of these Gentiles also became followers of Yeshua, these communities became an interesting mix of four different kinds of people: Jews who believed in Yeshua, Jews who did not, Gentiles who believed in Yeshua, and Gentiles who did not.[43] This obviously created further tensions.

Ephesus was an ancient Greek seaport on the Western coast of Ionia (in modern-day Turkey). During the classical Greek era it was one of the twelve cities of the Ionian League. The city was well-known for the Temple of Artemis/Diana (completed around 550 B.C.E.), which stood at the head of the harbor of Ephesus and was one of the Seven Wonders of the Ancient World. The city also had a large Jewish population, which is likely why Paul founded a community there and taught in Ephesus for three years (Acts 19). Paul also wrote an epistle to the community in Ephesus to address specific pastoral concerns. The city is also famous for being one of the seven congregations mentioned in the Book of Revelation (Rev. 2).

It was to Ephesus that John escaped after the destruction of Jerusalem, along with Yeshua's mother, Mary (Miriam), likely because of its large Jewish community and its established center of Yeshua-followers. It is believed he wrote his Gospel and letters in Ephesus, and where he is also believed to be buried.

The city was destroyed by the Goths in 263 and then rebuilt. However, following its resurrection, the city's importance as a

---

42. F.F. Bruce, *The Book of Acts* (The New International Commentary on the New Testament, Grand Rapids: Wm. B. Eerdmans, 1988), 203.
43. Nanos, *op. cit.,* 14-16, 73-74; et al.

commercial center declined as the harbor was slowly silted up by the Küçükmenderes River. Ephesus was the site of several 5th-century Christian Councils, but partially destroyed again by an earthquake in 614 C.E.

Given the strategic influence of Ephesus as a cultural and economic hub, Richard Bauckham proposes that John's gospel and letters would have therefore been intended for a wider audience beyond just those in his immediate sphere:

> All the gospels were written with the intention that they should circulate around all the churches ... According to all the evidence we have, the early Christian movement was not a scattering of relatively isolated, introverted communities, but a network of communities in constant, close communication with each other ... In addition, the evidence we have shows that Christian literature did in fact circulate around the churches very rapidly, while some evidence shows the deliberate launching of literature produced in one major church into general circulation around other churches.[44]

Although John's initial audience were those congregations directly affected by the pastoral issues addressed in his letters, he likely intended (or at least assumed) that the letters and his Gospel would also circulate more widely – geographically, socially, and demographically. This is evident in the way John includes references and language already familiar to a Jewish audience along with explanations for those less familiar.

Bauckham notes:

> John's account of Jesus at the Feast of Tabernacles (chapters 7-8) is considerably informed by the way this festival was celebrated in the first-century Jerusalem temple (which could

---

44. Bauckham, *op. cit.,* 114-115.

not be known [only] from the Old Testament). Readers with this knowledge would certainly benefit from it in their reading of these chapters, but the chapters are nevertheless quite intelligible to readers who lack this knowledge.[45]

In the past, many Johannine scholars argued that John's use of technical language was proof of a sectarian community who intended for these writings to remain insular. However, Bauckham argues that John actually wrote in an ingenious way which enfranchised and drew in anyone who read or heard his work: "Read sequentially, the Gospel leads its readers and hearers progressively into a greater understanding of its themes by initiating them step by step into its symbolic world."[46]

The Fourth Gospel does this by using technical terms and imagery, but often with a followed explanation. Here are a few examples from the first chapter alone (emphases mine):

- John 1:38 – "They said to him, Rabbi!" (which means "teacher!")

- John 1:41 – "We've found the *Mashiach*!" (The word means "one who has been anointed.")

- John 1:42 - He took him to Yeshua. Looking at him, Yeshua said, "You are *Shim'on Bar-Yochanan*; you will be known as *Kefa*." (The name means "rock.")

If John had intended for his gospel and letters to circulate only within a Jewish (and/or "insulated") audience there would be no need to give explanations for commonly understood words and ideas. Instead, as Bauckham demonstrates, "the author deliberately made his work accessible enough to outsiders for it to be read with profit by non-believers, Jewish or Gentile."[47]

---

45. Ibid., 122.
46. Ibid., 120.
47. Ibid., 13.

General Purpose

John wrote his brief epistles during a spiritually confusing time when there were conflicting theologies and behavioral concerns. According to Kruse, "the three letters appear to be interrelated, all dealing with one aspect or another of this dispute."[48] Although we do not know exactly all the underlying issues which prompted John's letters, we do know that he perceived these teaching to be dangerous, associating them with the "spirit of the anti-christ" (4:3). In this particular context, John uses the term not to refer to a supernatural agent, but to the false teaching because he is concerned others may be persuaded.

In the opening prologue of 1 John the author appeals to his authority (and apostolic authority in general) as an apostle – as a direct eyewitness who personally knew Yeshua and to whom authority was directly given. As Jobes confirms, "These letters insist that this apostolic testimony trumps any reinterpretation of Jesus by those who were not commissioned by him or who were far removed from personal knowledge of him."[49]

What is not exactly clear is the precise cause of the rift. The letters reflect a tension between two distinct views regarding Yeshua. Although the author of 1 John asserts that Yeshua "has come in the flesh" (4:2), others denied this claim. The general trend in Johannine scholarship has been to interpret this against the backdrop of Docetism (from the Greek word *dokeō*, meaning "to seem"), which taught that Yeshua only seemed to be human but was in reality fully, and only, divine.[50] The correct theological balance, of course, is that Yeshua is both.

---

48. Kruse, *op. cit.,* 1.
49. Jobes, *op. cit.,* 23.
50. Murray, *op. cit., 448.*

Kruse summarizes, "Whatever the influences that affected them were, they all led to a deemphasizing of the incarnation and vicarious death of Christ and a concomitant deemphasizing of the commands of Christ, especially the command to love one another."[51]

Although it is tempting to imagine the identities of those who broke away, their exact teachings, or motivations for doing so, we must also acknowledge that we cannot accurately assume a precise motivation for John's epistles, especially when the letters themselves do not directly identify the exact issues they are refuting. Therefore, Jobes cautions:

> The major themes of right belief about Jesus, a right attitude toward sin, and interpersonal relationships characterized by love are clear, but why the author has chosen to discuss these particular topics is not. He reinforces his authority as a bearer of the apostolic teaching about the revelation of God in Jesus Christ, which implies that the source of truth about God in Christ was in some dispute. But the author writes with the intent of a pastor to care for his people rather than as an apologist to argue directly against those who have left the Johannine church(es) … It is important to emphasize the fact that, in spite of this, the real aim of the Epistle is not exclusively, or even primarily, polemical.[52]

Although John wrote to address particular pastoral concerns, his letters also provide wider and significant contributions on a number of key theological issues and themes, which remain relevant into the present day.

---

51. Kruse, *op. cit.,* 20.
52. Jobes, *op. cit.,* 23.

The World of John: Historical Context

There is now overwhelming scholarly consensus on the "Jewishness of Jesus" and the thoroughly Jewish world within which we must read the New Testament.[53] This hermeneutic should also be understood to extend to the apostle John as well. He was a faithful Jewish follower of the Messiah who understood his faith from within an entirely Jewish context. This is true for all of the earliest Jewish believers and is the framework within which the New Testament must be read.

Furthermore, John wrote his letters during a tumultuous time (in many ways). In the late first-century, after Jerusalem was conquered by the Romans and the Temple razed, Jews were expelled from the city, and the center of Yeshua-faith (along with all of Judaism) was thrown into tumultuous chaos. Over two and a half million Jews were killed as a result of war, famine and disease. Over a million Jews were exiled to all parts of the Roman Empire, over 100,000 Jews were sold as slaves, and Jews were killed and tortured in gladiatorial "games" and pagan celebrations.[54]

Until Jerusalem was destroyed it was still the primary spiritual hub for the nascent Yeshua-believing community and its leadership. After the city's destruction, however, the community and its leadership were scattered and forced to flee to other regions of the Roman Empire. This was ultimately the underlying cause behind the scattering of the disciples.

---

53. See further: Amy-Jill Levine, *The Misunderstood Jew* (New York: Harper Collins, 2006); David Flusser, *The Sage from Galilee* (Grand Rapids: Eerdmans Publishing, 2007); James Charlesworth, Ed. *Jesus' Jewishness* (New York: Crossroad, 1997); Geza Vermes, *Jesus the Jew* (Minneapolis: Fortress Press, 1981); etc.

54. Ancient History Encyclopedia. "The Great Jewish Revolt of 66 C.E." Accessed March 3, 2019 - https://www.ancient.eu/article/823/the-great-jewish-revolt-of-66-C.E./. Also see - https://ohr.edu/1088.

We cannot underestimate the impact the Temple's destruction and the subsequent expulsions had on the development of Yeshua-faith. This catastrophic event, along with Roman persecution and the eventual deaths of the original apostles, created a vacuum within which heretical theologies and behaviors began creeping into the communities, and became a constant battle reflected in the pastoral letters and beyond.[55]

Hellenistic or Judean?

It was once argued that the Johannine corpus was written from an entirely Hellenistic worldview and perspective, drawing upon language and imagery from Greek paganism and other wider influences. Although that argument has long been shattered, it is still common for people to read and interpret John with shades of this assumption.

Furthermore, the standard approach has also assumed that John's writings are inconsistent with Jewish faith and identity, representing a break with Judaism. Many even argue they are "anti-Jewish." For example, Peter J. Tomson contends:

> The Gospel of John ... is continually about the 'Jews' and certainly has a Jewish background, but due to its strong antagonism towards the Jews and the law, it should not be called Jewish but anti-Jewish.[56]

Tomson further argues that John's portrayal of Judaism and even his depiction of Yeshua's relationship to Jews and Judaism is a negative one:

---

55. For example, see my work on Jude (Clarksville: Lederer, 2014).
56. Peter J. Tomson, *'If This Be From Heaven...'* (Sheffield: Sheffield Academic Press, 2001), 336

- "In all events it is clear that, according to the fourth Gospel, Jesus deliberately and knowingly transgresses Shabbat." He even acknowledges, "Such a message is heard nowhere else in the New Testament …"[57]

- "It appears that, from the perspective of the Gospel, the appeal to Moses and the law belongs to the past and functions only polemically."[58]

- "Within the totally unique thought world of the Johannine milieu, not only the Jewish law but also the name 'Jews' receives a negative connotation."[59]

- *"The fourth Gospel views the Jewish people to whom Jesus speaks from the outside* (italics his)."[60]

Unfortunately, Tomson is hardly alone in this interpretation of the Johannine corpus. Raimo Hakola, for example, asserts:

> John's ambivalent attitude toward Jewishness and some fierce attacks against characters who seem to represent some types of Jewish Christians indicate that it may be misleading to label the Johannine Christians as Jewish Christians, even though there is no way of denying that the roots of these Christians were firmly on Jewish ground.[61]

He further argues:

> John's alienation from the basics of Jewishness and some passing but virulent attacks against Christian believers who

---

57. Ibid., 318.
58. Ibid., 321.
59. Ibid., 322.
60. Ibid., 324.
61. Raimo Hakola. "The Johannine Community as Jewish Christians? Some Problems in Current Scholarly Consensus." *Jewish Christianity Reconsidered.* Ed. Matt Jackson-McCabe. (Minneapolis: Fortress Press, 2007), 181.

did not see any contradiction between faith in Jesus and the observance of Jewish practices suggest that John should not be placed on a Jewish-Christian trajectory of early Christianity. ... [T]he Johannine writer was well aware of his drift away from Jewishness. John and his community no longer understood themselves in terms of Jewish identity."[62]

Such "anti-Jewish" accusations are regularly employed toward Johannine literature, however what exactly is implied by the label varies between scholars. A wealth of additional examples could be given, but these should suffice in demonstrating that John's writings have largely been interpreted though this kind of a supersessionist lens.

When there are positive Jewish representations within John's writings, they are often ignored, dismissed, or explained away. For instance, Tomson wrestles with how to reconcile John's regular references to so many Jewish festivals and concludes, "The Gospel of John as a whole evidences great aversion to Jewish ritual. To the extent that there indeed is an interest in the feasts, this must have belonged to an early stage in the development of the Gospel."[63]

Such readings completely ignore and miss what we know about John and the earliest disciples, especially if we conclude that the apostle John, the son of Zebedee, is indeed the author of the Fourth gospel and the Johannine letters. John was a Galilean Jew and a close disciple of Yeshua. Even John's eventual settling in Ephesus must be viewed in light of the destruction of Jerusalem and the Temple, and the expulsion of Jews from the city. We must also consider the choice of Ephesus in light of its large Jewish

---

62. Ibid., 199.
63. Tomson, *op. cit.*, 300.

population and concentration of Yeshua-followers. The entire context is Jewish. Therefore, it does not make sense to believe that along with John's fleeing from Jerusalem he also abandoned his commitment to Jewish life, faith, worldview, and understanding of "The Way."[64]

To truly make sense of John's writings we must recognize and embrace the thoroughly Jewish milieu out of which they emerged and were informed. Even when that is difficult. Rather than simply concluding these texts are "anti-Jewish," these conflicts should be read as "intra-Jewish" – as one committed Jewish person speaking to and about other Jewish people and issues (often vehemently). These kids of intra-group dynamics are wrought with polemical and antagonistic language. However, we must keep in mind that John, along with all the other New Testament authors, are still arguing for their particular interpretation of Judaism against competing alternatives.[65]

As Eli Lizorkin-Eyzenberg notes:

> In John, as in other parts of the Bible, Jesus has some very hard things to say ... After all, harsh rhetoric is also present in the so-called "most Jewish" of all the Gospels, the Gospel of Matthew (Matt. 23) and is consistent with the standard of speech of the Israelite prophets. Just begin reading Isaiah or Amos (among many others) and you will easily see my point.[66]

---

64. The earliest followers of Yeshua referred to themselves as followers of The Way - HaDerekh (Acts 9:2; 19:9; 22:4), because they understood their form of Judaism as *the way* to correctly live and understand being Jewish. The term was also employed by the Qumran community.

65. Nanos, *op. cit.,* 4.

66. Eli Lizorkin-Eyzenberg, *The Jewish Gospel of John* (Tel Mond: Israel Study Center, 2015), viii.

He further writes:

> You see, other than reading the abundance of what seem to be anti-Jewish statements, this Gospel also boasts a large number of pro-Jewish stories and statements that are in fact not present in the other Gospels. Only in this Gospel are the Jews actually called "his own." (John 1:11b) Only in this Gospel Jesus meets the Samaritan woman and tells her "Salvation is from the Jews." (John 4:22) Only in this Gospel Jesus is said to be buried according to the customs of "the Jews" (John 19:40) – this too is a powerful statement of belonging. And as a final example, only in this Gospel is Jesus portrayed as experiencing emotional pain, together with the Jews, when he mourns Lazarus. (John 11:33)[67]

Although John's criticisms can often seem harsh, they must also be viewed within a wider context of Jewish prophetic nuance and in-group dynamics, without presupposing a particular bias. According to Nanos:

> Where New Testament scholarship is concerned, the literature can now be read as Jewish correspondence, written by and for Jews and gentiles concerned with the Jewish context of their new faith in Jesus as the Jewish Messiah who had come *first* to restore the Jewish people, and *also* to bring salvation to non-Jewish people as the Savior of the world. It is now possible to approach the contingent nature of these texts without presupposing an anti-Jewish bias on the part of the writers, or the audience they addressed [italics his].[68]

---

67. Ibid., x.
68. Nanos, *op. cit.,* 4.

The Thoroughly Jewish Context of John's Theology

We must also affirm the growing call to read and interpret the theology of the Johannine corpus from within a Jewish contextual framework. As Bauckham explains:

> The roots of John's particular modes of thought and expression lie in Palestinian Jewish and Jewish-Christian tradition ... The turning point in Johannine scholarship's increasing emphasis on the Jewishness of the Gospel came with the publication of major texts from the Dead Sea Scrolls, which apparently revealed a world of Palestinian Jewish thought with parallels precisely to those aspects of Johannine theology – especially its 'dualism' – that had been thought to require Hellenistic or Gnostic sources.[69]

Bauckham further emphasizes:

> The monotheistic theme in John is far from merely apologetic or polemical, designed to show, against Jewish objections to Christology, that divine Christology is not incompatible with Jewish monotheism ... Thus, without contradicting or rejecting any of the existing features of Jewish monotheism, the Fourth Gospel redefines it as Christological monotheism, a form of monotheism in which the relationship of Jesus the Son to his Father is integral to who the one God is.[70]

The more we understand about the Second Temple period and early Jewish interpretive traditions, the more we are able to appreciate John's theology and its consistency with broader Messianic developments within Judaism. This is especially evident in relation to John's use of the term Logos throughout his writings. Rather

---

69. Bauckham, *op. cit.,* 22-23.
70. Ibid., 252.

than drawing on the often assumed Hellenistic use and imagery for this term, John's understanding is rooted in Jewish sources and thought. As John Ronning astutely asserts:

> John's decision to call Jesus "the Word," the Logos (ὁ λόγος), was influenced by the Targums, the Aramaic translations of the Hebrew Scriptures, many or most of which were prepared for recitation in the synagogue after the reading of the Hebrew text. In hundreds of cases in these Targums, where the [Masoretic Text] refers to God, the corresponding Targum passage refers to the divine *Word*. Considered against this background, calling Jesus "the Word" is a way of identifying him with the God of Israel. … [U]nderstanding the Logos title as based on the Targums is crucial to understanding not only John's Prologue, but the body of the Gospel as well, for if we understand the Logos as a divine title, we can see that John's statements about the Word (the Word was with God, the Word was God, and the Word became flesh) presage themes throughout the Gospel.[71]

Daniel Boyarin likens John's Prologue in the Gospel to early Midrash[72] and proposes that it is "conceivable to see the Prologue, together with its Logos doctrine, as a Jewish text through and through rather than, as it has often been read, a 'Hellenized corruption' of Judaism."[73] In late antiquity there were plenty of Jews who "firmly held theological doctrines of a second God,

---

71. John Ronning, *The Jewish Targums and John's Logos Theology* (Peabody: Hendrickson, 2010), 1.
72. Midrash is an interpretive method and a creative body of literature that seeks to fill-in gaps and answer questions within Scripture. It does so through delving into the deeper meaning of words, finding similarities with other biblical passages, and using Hebrew word plays, numerology, and parables.
73. Daniel Boyarin, *Borderlines: The Partition of Judaeo-Christianity* (Philadelphia: University of Pennsylvania Press, 2004), 31.

variously called Logos, Memra, Sophia, Metatron, or Yahoel; indeed perhaps most Jews did so."[74]

Boyarin argues:

> The Logos of the Prologue – like the theological Logos in general . . . is the product of a scriptural reading of Genesis 1 and Proverbs 8 together. This reading will bear out my conclusion that nothing in Logos theology as a doctrine of God indicates or even implies a particularly Christian as opposed to generally Jewish, including Christian kerygma ... we must pay attention to the formal characteristics of Midrash as a mode of reading Scripture ... This hermeneutical practice is founded on a theological notion of the oneness of Scripture as a self-interpreting text.[75]

Boyarin further emphasizes, "Gaps are not filled with philosophical ideas but with allusions to or citations of other texts. The first five verses of the Prologue to the Fourth Gospel fit this form nearly perfectly."[76] He points to wisdom texts and hymns as aids in exploring this hypothesis further, noting that Philo[77] identifies Sophia and Logos as a single entity. Furthermore, within certain Wisdom texts, Proverbs 8 became important in the Jewish interpretive tradition of Genesis 1.[78] Demonstrating how Sophia (wisdom) became a personified midrashic tool to decipher other passages, he uses an illustration from Baruch 3:37 to illustrate an incarnation of God's pre-existent Wisdom: "Afterward she appeared upon the earth and lived among men." Using midrashic method, Boyarin argues that it is

---

74. Ibid., 92.
75. Ibid., 95.
76. Ibid., 95.
77. Philo Judaeus, also known as Philo of Alexandria, was a Hellenistic Jewish philosopher who lived in Alexandria, in the Roman province of Egypt. He used philosophical allegory to harmonize Jewish scripture with Greek philosophy (see the glossary for more information).
78. Boyarin, *op. cit.,* 95.

not so unusual to arrive at an interpretation of "God's extraordinary incarnation of his son, the Logos."[79]

Expanding specifically upon the work of Daniel Boyarin, Carl Kinbar asserts that in addition to "tracing the Second Temple and early rabbinic uses of the Greek word *logos* [λόγος] and the Aramaic *memra* [מֵימְרָא] - both meaning, 'a spoken word'" ... we can also introduce "uses of the Hebrew *dibbur* [דִּיבּוּר], also meaning 'a spoken word.' Since logos, memra, and dibbur share highly overlapping semantic domains."[80]

According to Kinbar:

> [D]ibbur is used of a hypostatic Word in a number of midrashim attributed to rabbis of the second through fifth centuries C.E. These midrashim were then included by the author-editors of midrash collections assembled from at least the fifth through ninth centuries, indicating that some of the sages of those later centuries retained the idea of a hypostatic Word serving as a mediator between God and Israel.[81]

More on this could be said, but clearly, John's conception of the Logos is predicated upon his "combination of Jewish messianic soteriology with equally Jewish Logos theology in the figure of Jesus."[82]

Genre, Structure and Language

John composed his epistles in Greek, a language that allowed them to be widely circulated across the broadest demographic and geographical spectrum, as it was the primary trade and cultural

---

79. Ibid., 97.
80. Carl Kinbar, Addendum to "Israel, Interpretation, and the Knowledge of God." A paper presented at the 2010 Hashivenu forum, Agoura Hills, CA, 24.
81. Ibid., 24.
82. Boyarin, *op. cit.,* 105.

language of the time. And when John cites passages from the Tanakh, or makes use of Tanakh-language, he quotes from the Septuagint (LXX), the widely-circulated authoritative translation of the Hebrew bible into Greek.[83] This would make sense given his immediate audience in the Diaspora. It could also have been a matter of convenience, since John was not a native Greek speaker. When quoting Tanakh passages in Greek it may have been easier for John to cite those passages from a source already in Greek rather than produce his own translation.

2 and 3 John are real letters, featuring the common characteristic of ancient epistles. However, 1 John is neither a letter nor a more formal epistle[84] as it lacks the tradition features of genuine correspondence.[85] Other stylistic differences have led many to argue that 1 John may have originally been a sermon or tract. This would not be unusual, as other biblical books are also believed to have been delivered orally before being circulated in writing.

1 John is intended for a specific audience and directed to a particular situation, with a gentle pastoral tone. 2 John is a letter, written to a specific congregation(s), to warn about the false teachers described in 1 John, and to encourage them to remain faithful. 3 John, however, was a personal letter addressed to a specific individual, Gaius, and speaks of hospitality.[86]

More specific discussions of structure will be handled in the introductory paragraphs to each epistle.

---

83. For more information, refer to the entry "Septuagint" in the Glossary.
84. Thomas F. Johnson, *1,2 & 3 John* (Understanding the Bible Commentary Series, Grand Rapids: Baker Books, 1993), 13.
85. Marianne Meye Thompson, *1-3 John* (The IVP New Testament Commentary Series, Downers Grove: IVP Academic, 1992), 18.
86. Ibid., 18-19.

Canonical Order: Implications of Location

Another critical issue we must consider is what role the order of the books in the New Testament play in our conception of John's letters. In the current order of the canon John's letters are stuck all the way in the back, towards the end. But what if John's letters were not in the back, but rather placed toward the front - after the Gospels and before Paul's letters? Would it then change how we read and interpret them? Would we maybe perceive them as being more relevant and important if they were closer to the front?

In actuality, this may originally have been the case. In the three oldest canonical orders of the New Testament, from codices *Vaticanus, Sinaiticus and Alexandrinus,* two of them place the "General Epistles," which include 1-3 John, after the Gospels and Acts, and before Paul's letters:[87]

---

87. The below chart: John W. Miller, *How the Bible Came to Be* (New York: Paulist Press, 2004), 57 *(emphases and dates mine).*

Codex Vaticanus (c. 4th century)	Codex Sinaiticus (c. mid-4th century)	Codex Alexandrinus (c. 5th century)
Matthew	Matthew	Matthew (25:6-28:20 only)
Mark	Mark	Mark
Luke	Luke	Luke
John	John	John (6:50-8:52 missing)
Acts	Romans	Acts
James	1 Corinthians	James
1 Peter	2 Corinthians	1 Peter
2 Peter	Galatians	2 Peter
1 JOHN	Ephesians	**1 JOHN**
2 JOHN	Philippians	**2 JOHN**
3 JOHN	Colossians	**3 JOHN**
Jude	1 Thessalonians	Jude
Romans	2 Thessalonians	Romans
1 Corinthians	Hebrews	1 Corinthians
2 Corinthians	1 Timothy	2 Corinthians (4:13-12:6 missing)
Galatians	2 Timothy	Galatians
Ephesians	Titus	Ephesians
Philippians	Philemon	Philippians
Colossians	Acts	Colossians
1 Thessalonians	James	1 Thessalonians
2 Thessalonians	1 Peter	2 Thessalonians
Hebrews (1:1-9:14)	2 Peter	Hebrews
	1 JOHN	1 Timothy
(Ending lost, including the Pastorals)	**2 JOHN**	2 Timothy
	3 JOHN	Titus
	Jude	Philemon
	Revelation	Revelation
	Barnabas	1 Clement (2-12:5)
	Shepherd of Hermas	

This observation has tremendous implications for how we read and interpret the letters of John. The books were placed in a specific order to highlight a particular narrative structure. This is one reason why the Jewish and Christian canons of the Hebrew Scriptures differ. The books are the same, but placed in different orders, thereby stressing different narrative arcs. In a canonical structure which places John's letters much earlier in the order, greater prominence is placed on the books and their relation to all the others. They become tools to thereby interpret the epistles which follow.

Which leads us to ask ourselves, what if we considered John's letters as prominently as Paul's many letters? This would dramatically change the way we not only view John's epistles but could even alter the way we view other letters within the New Testament as well. However, to discover these implications, we must delve further into the texts themselves.

1 JOHN

John's three letters were written during a tumultuous time for the followers of Yeshua. It was the end of first century, Jerusalem was recently destroyed, the Temple razed, and the Jerusalem community of Yeshua-followers (and its leadership), along with all other Jews, were forced to flee, scattered across the Roman Empire. As a result, coupled together with the deaths of the earliest disciples and eyewitnesses of Yeshua, there was a lot of spiritual confusion.

As discussed in the Introduction, the three Johannine Epistles are traditionally ascribed to *Yochanan ben Zavdai* (John the son of Zebedee), who was one of Yeshua's twelve closest disciples. Following the destruction of Jerusalem (around 70 C.E.), John fled with *Miriam* (Mary), Yeshua's mother, to Ephesus where he composed his Gospel and Letters, and where he lived out the rest of his life (he died around 100 C.E.).[1]

John wrote his letters (c.85-95) to confront a split over conflicting theologies and behavioral concerns. Certain individuals broke away from the network of congregations under John's care and authority and were traveling around attempting to influence

---

1. For more about John, Ephesus and the context of the letters, see the Introduction.

33

others with their false teachings. John's primary concern was to both encourage and warn all those who looked to him for guidance.

According to Colin G. Kruse, "the three letters appear to be interrelated, all dealing with one aspect or another of this dispute."[2] There seems to have been a tension over two distinct views regarding Yeshua. Although the author of 1 John asserts that Yeshua "has come in the flesh" (4:2), others denied this claim. The general trend in Johannine scholarship has been to interpret this conflict against the backdrop of Docetism (from the Greek word *dokeō*, meaning "to seem"), which taught that Yeshua only *seemed* to be human but was in reality fully, and only, divine.[3] Kruse summarizes, "whatever the influences that affected them were, they all led to a deemphasizing of the incarnation and vicarious death of Christ and a concomitant deemphasizing of the commands of Christ, especially the command to love one another."[4]

Although it is tempting imagine all the various scenarios and circumstances behind the rift, we must be careful to acknowledge that we cannot accurately discern a more precise stimulus for John's epistles, especially since the letters themselves do not directly identify in further detail the exact issues they are refuting. Therefore, as Karen H. Jobes cautions:

> The major themes of right belief about Jesus, a right attitude toward sin, and interpersonal relationships characterized by love are clear, but why the author has chosen to discuss these particular topics is not. He reinforces his authority as a bearer of the apostolic teaching about the revelation of God in Jesus Christ, which implies that the source of truth about God in Christ was in some dispute. But the author writes

---

2. Kruse, *op. cit.*, 1.
3. Murray, *op. cit.*, *448*.
4. Kruse, *op. cit.*, 20.

with the intent of a pastor to care for his people rather than as an apologist to argue directly against those who have left the Johannine church(es) ... It is important to emphasize the fact that, in spite of this, the real aim of the Epistle is not exclusively, or even primarily, polemical.[5]

Although John wrote to address particular pastoral concerns, he also wrote to provide hope, encouragement, and guidance. His letters also provide significant contributions on a number of key theological issues and themes which remain relevant to the present day.

Language, Genre and Structure

John composed his epistles in Greek, a language that allowed them to be widely circulated across the broadest demographic and geographical spectrum. And when John cites passages from the Tanakh, or makes use of Tanakh-language, he quotes from the Septuagint (LXX), the widely-circulated authoritative translation of the Hebrew bible into Greek.[6] This would make sense given his immediate audience in the Diaspora.

1 John was initially intended for a specific audience (his immediate community) and dealt with a particular situation (the false teachers). We must also keep in mind that although we often refer to 1 John as a letter, it is really more of a treatise or written sermon, and lacks the traditional elements of a true letter (unlike 2 and 3 John). The structure of 1 John suggests the author intended it to be read or performed aloud, and was most likely a sermon originally communicated to the author's home congregation and then circulated to outlying congregations.[7]

---

5. Jobes, *op. cit.*, 23.
6. For more information, refer to the entry "Septuagint" in the Glossary.
7. Jobes, *op. cit.*, 37.

According to Jobes, "modern analyses using various methodologies have shown that 1 John is a carefully crafted work."[8] It also has a very unique structure, as she explains:

> The structure of 1 John is difficult to outline because its thought is circular rather than linear. It returns to the same intertwined themes – sin, love, and sound Christology – again and again, developing each further in light of what has been said of the other two.[9]

Kruse confirms this unique style:

> As a piece of epideictic rhetoric, 1 John ... revisits the same themes over and over, each time amplifying them further. For this reason commentators have a great difficulty describing the structure of this letter. Frequently one reads comments about the repetitive nature of the letter and its spiraling structure.[10]

Thomas F. Johnson echoes similar sentiments:

> The author prefers to express himself in contrasts in order to state or to clarify his teaching. These motifs of contrast are interrelated. They overlap one another and present the author's doctrinal and ethical concerns in a variety of ways. Repetition, with and without nuance, is a prominent stylistic characteristic. The author's language has a way of doubling back on itself, as in a spiral, before it moves ahead into a new expression of thought.[11]

Repetition and returning amplification are methods not only found in Greco-Roman rhetorical structure, but also found in biblical and rabbinic texts. Hebrew often uses repetition or the

---

8. Ibid., 39.
9. Ibid., 38.
10. Kruse, *op. cit.,* 31.
11. Thomas F. Johnson, *1, 2 & 3 John* (Understanding the Bible Commentary Series, Grand Rapids: Baker Books, 1993), 13.

doubling-up of words and phrases as a form of emphasis. John is clearly drawing upon Greco-Roman rhetorical structure in his careful crafting of 1 John. I don't deny this. However, we should also consider what role John's biblical familiarity and Semitic background played in its composition.

Furthermore, although 1 John was originally communicated to the author's own community (and immediate vicinity), as the influence of those who broke-away spread, John may have found the need to communicate his warning to a broader audience. Therefore, as Marianne Meye Thompson proposes:

> It is possible that 2 John served as a cover letter, sent along with 1 John, to include personal greetings from the Elder to a specific congregation in his care. It is also possible that 1 and 2 John were intended for different audiences: 1 John was circulated in the Elder's immediate vicinity, while 2 John was sent to those at a distance, whom the Elder could contact only by letter (v.12) or by messenger (v.4). In any case, it is safe to say that the two letters illumine each other and are so obviously written with the same situation in view that each may be used to interpret the other.[12]

John's Jewish Context

It is vital we keep the Jewish context of John in mind as we study his writings. The more we understand the Second Temple period and early Jewish interpretive traditions, the more we are able to appreciate John's theology and its consistency with broader Messianic developments within Judaism. This is especially evident, for example, in John's regular use of the term Logos throughout his writings.

---

12. Thompson, *op. cit.,* 150.

Outline of 1 John[13]

---

13. Adapted from Thompson, *op. cit.,* 131-32.

1 JOHN
CHAPTER 1

vv. 1-4 - Prologue

---

1 The Word, which gives life!
He existed from the beginning.
We have heard him, we have seen him with our eyes,
we have contemplated him, we have touched him with our
hands!
2 The life appeared, and we have seen it.
We are testifying to it and announcing it to you - eternal life!
He was with the Father, and he appeared to us.
3 What we have seen and heard, we are proclaiming to you;
so that you too may have fellowship with us.
Our fellowship is with the Father and with his Son, Yeshua the
Messiah.
4 We are writing these things so that our joy may be complete.

As we read through these opening verses we readily notice similarities with the Prologue in John's Gospel. The Word, which gives life and existed from the beginning, is Yeshua.

It has often been assumed that John wrote from an entirely Hellenistic worldview and perspective. However, the better we understand the Second Temple period, the more we are able to appreciate John's theology and its consistency with broader Messianic developments within Early Judaism. This is especially true, for example, concerning John's use of the term *Logos* throughout his writings (the Greek word translated as *"the Word"*). Rather than drawing upon the often assumed Hellenistic use and imagery for this term, John's understanding is actually rooted in Jewish sources and thought. According to John Ronning:

> John's decision to call Jesus "the Word," the Logos (ὁ λόγος), was influenced by the Targums, the Aramaic translations of the Hebrew Scriptures, many or most of which were prepared for recitation in the synagogue after the reading of the Hebrew text. In hundreds of cases in these Targums, where the [Masoretic Text] refers to God, the corresponding Targum passage refers to the divine *Word*. Considered against this background, calling Jesus "the Word" is a way of identifying him with the God of Israel. … [U]nderstanding the Logos title as based on the Targums is crucial to understanding not only John's Prologue, but the body of the Gospel as well, for if we understand the Logos as a divine title, we can see that John's statements about the Word … presage themes throughout the Gospel.[1]

This is true of both Prologues (in 1 John and the Fourth Gospel).

Daniel Boyarin likens John's Prologue to early Midrash and proposes that it is "conceivable to see the Prologue, together with its Logos doctrine, as a Jewish text through and through rather than, as it has often been read, a 'Hellenized corruption' of Judaism."[2] He explains:

---

1. Ronning, *op. cit.,* 1.
2. Boyarin, *Borderlines, op. cit.,* 31.

The Logos of the Prologue – like the theological Logos in general . . . is the product of a scriptural reading of Genesis 1 and Proverbs 8 together. This reading will bear out my conclusion that nothing in Logos theology as a doctrine of God indicates or even implies a particularly Christian as opposed to generally Jewish, including Christian kerygma ... we must pay attention to the formal characteristics of Midrash as a mode of reading Scripture ... This hermeneutical practice is founded on a theological notion of the oneness of Scripture as a self-interpreting text.[3]

Boyarin points to wisdom texts and hymns as aids in exploring his hypothesis further, noting that Philo[4] identifies Sophia and Logos as a single entity. Furthermore, within certain Wisdom texts, Proverbs 8 became important in the Jewish interpretive tradition of Genesis 1.[5] Demonstrating further how Sophia (wisdom) became a personified midrashic tool to decipher other passages, he uses an illustration from Baruch 3:37 to illustrate an incarnation of God's pre-existent Wisdom: "Afterward she appeared upon the earth and lived among men." Therefore, using midrashic method, Boyarin contends that it is not so unusual to arrive at an interpretation of "God's extraordinary incarnation of his son, the Logos."[6]

According to Boyarin, Logos theology was commonly held by Jews of all stripes (not just "Jewish Christians"), and defines the term as:

A doctrine that between God and the world, there is a second divine entity, God's Word (Logos) or God's Wisdom, who

---

3. Ibid., 95.
4. Philo Judaeus, also known as Philo of Alexandria, was a Hellenistic Jewish philosopher who lived in Alexandria, in the Roman province of Egypt. He used philosophical allegory to harmonize Jewish scripture with Greek philosophy (see the glossary for more information).
5. Boyarin, *Borderlines, op. cit.,* 95.
6. Ibid., 97.

mediates between the fully transcendent Godhead and the material world. This doctrine was widely held by Jews in the pre-Christian era and after the beginnings of Christianity was widely held and widely contested in Christian circles. By the fourth century, Jews who held such a doctrine and Christians who rejected it were defined as 'neither Jews nor Christians' but heretics.[7]

Throughout the rabbinic period, there is evidence of a vital form of Judaism that was not only extra-rabbinic but which the Rabbis explicitly named a heresy - the belief in 'Two Powers in Heaven,' or in our terms, Logos theology.[8] Most Jews possibly resisted efforts to appropriate the Logos exclusively for Christianity, and additionally detested the efforts of those Rabbis who sought to corroborate that exclusion. For those Jews, even in Israel, the *Logos* (referred to as *memra,* or 'word' in Aramaic) remained an important theological being.[9]

The word *Memra* (מֵמְרָא) is often used interchangeably with God in Aramaic texts. Boyarin confirms, "historical investigation suggests that in the first two centuries C.E., the *Memra* was not a mere name, but an actual divine entity functioning as a mediator."[10] Over time Logos theology was rejected largely because it became associated as "Christian," along with any sort of binitarian conception of God (let alone trinitarianism). This rejection became an ultimate touchstone of Rabbinic Judaism.

---

7. Ibid., 30-31.
8. Boyarin emphasizes, "There is no reason to imagine, however, that 'rabbinic Judaism' ever became the popular hegemonic form of Jewish religiosity among the 'People of the Land,' and there is good reason to believe the opposite" (p. 89). Rather, Yavnean development evolved over time, which he explores further in chapter 7.
9. Ibid., 89.
10. Daniel Boyarin. "Logos, A Jewish Word: John's Prologue as Midrash," *The Jewish Annotated New Testament*, Ed. Amy-Jill Levine and Marc Zvi Brettler (New York: Oxford, 2011), 546-547.

Carl Kinbar astutely adds that John's underlying conception of the term Logos is not limited to Aramaic or Greek texts, but draws upon Hebrew sources as well. By "tracing the Second Temple and early rabbinic uses of the Greek word *logos* [λόγος] and the Aramaic *memra* [מֵמְרָא] - both meaning, 'a spoken word'" … we can also introduce "uses of the Hebrew *dibbur* [דִּיבּוּר], also meaning 'a spoken word.' Since logos, memra, and dibbur share highly overlapping semantic domains."[11]

Kinbar elaborates:

> [D]ibbur is used of a hypostatic Word in a number of midrashim attributed to rabbis of the second through fifth centuries C.E. These midrashim were then included by the author-editors of midrash collections assembled from at least the fifth through ninth centuries, indicating that some of the sages of those later centuries retained the idea of a hypostatic Word serving as a mediator between God and Israel.[12]

The root of *Dibbur* is *Davar* (דָּבָר).[13] *HaDavar* – literally, "the Word," is the way Hebrew translations of John render the word *Logos*:

John 1:1

בְּרֵשִׁית הָיָה הַדָּבָר וְהַדָּבָר הָיָה אֶת הָאֱלֹהִים וֵאלֹהִים הָיָה הַדָּבָר:

B'reshit hayah ha-davar v'ha-davar hayah et ha-Elohim v'Elohim hayah ha-davar.

---

11. Carl Kinbar, Addendum to "Israel, Interpretation, and the Knowledge of God." A paper presented at the 2010 Hashivenu forum, Agoura Hills, CA, 24.
12. Ibid., 24.
13. As with other Semitic languages, words are conjugated from three letter roots. *Devar* (דְּבָר) is also the word often used in Hebrew translations of the NT for the Greek word *Logos* (λόγος).

In the beginning was the Word, and the Word was with God, and the Word was God.

The great 19th century Jewish believer, Rabbi Yechiel Tzvi Lichtenstein, in his monumental Hebrew commentary on the New Testament, [14] expounds:

> The word *Davar*, or in Greek *Logos* ... is a known concept among the sages of Israel, as we see in the Aramaic Targumim, and also in Targum Jonathan ben Uziel who lived in the same generation as Yeshua of Nazareth, where it uses the words *Memra of Adonai* or just *Memra*. [15]

Lichtenstein then cites the RaMbaM's (Maimonides)[16] commentary on Genesis 46:1 *(Parashat Vayigash)*, where the RaMbaM notes that where the Torah uses the phrase *"Davar HaShem"* the Aramaic *targumim* use the phrase *"Memra."* Lichtenstein then continues and adds:

> The phrase 'the Word was God' is paralleled in verse 14, and the words 'the Word was made flesh' imply that he was God before time. This is the reason Philo used the term 'second god' because according to his *middot*[17] and his nature he resembled HaShem, as it states in Philippians 2:6, he was in the form of HaShem and equal to him.[18]

More on this could easily be said, but clearly, John's conception of the Logos is predicated upon his "combination of Jewish messianic

---

14. Originally published in consecutive volumes between 1891-1904 in Leipzig, Germany.
15. Yechiel Tzvi Lichtenstein, *Sugiyot Nivcharot B'sefer HaBrit HaChadashah* (Jerusalem: Keren Ahavah Meshichit, 2002), 111-112 [translation mine].
16. RaMbaM is a Hebrew acronym for "Rabbi Moshe ben Maimon," also known as Maimonides, who was one of the greatest Torah commentators of the Middle Ages. See the glossary for more information.
17. Attributes. The concept is derived from the attributes of God described in Exodus 34.
18. Lichtenstein, *op. cit.*, 111-112.

soteriology with equally Jewish Logos theology in the figure of Jesus."[19] John was exhorting his audience using language and concepts they were likely already familiar with (especially if they were Jewish). However, there is one key development in John's theology, as Keener notes:

> Although philosophers and Jewish teachers alike spoke of the divine Word, none of them spoke of the Word's becoming human. By saying that Jesus' witnesses had touched and felt him, John indicates that Jesus had been fully human; he was not simply a divine apparition …[20]

However, in light of the above discussion, as Boyarin argued, it is not so unusual to arrive at an interpretation of "God's extraordinary incarnation of his son, the Logos."[21] John's theology was a natural progression – a logical next step – in Jewish Logos theology, and in describing exactly who he understood Yeshua to be based on direct experience and knowledge.

Mark S. Kinzer summarizes this discussion nicely:

> While the enfleshment of the *Memra* (Word) is a new and unique event, it should nonetheless be viewed in continuity with what precedes it – as a concentrated and intensified form of the divine presence that accompanies Israel throughout its historical journey. Thus, contrary to the common Christian canonical narrative, the divinity of Yeshua can be seen not as a radical rupture and disjunction in the story but as a continuation and elevation of the process initiated long ago.[22]

---

19. Boyarin, *Borderlines, op. cit.,* 105.
20. Craig S. Keener, *The IVP Bible Background Commentary: New Testament* (Downers Grove: IVP Academic, 1993), 737.
21. Ibid., 97.
22. Mark S. Kinzer, *Israel's Messiah and the People of God.* Ed. Jennifer M. Rosner. (Eugene: Cascade Press, 2011), 104.

The Word, which gives life! ... eternal life! – Unpacking what John exactly means by "life," Kinzer writes:

> In the apostolic tradition ... "life" refers to a gift bestowed in the future, in the world to come (Matthew 7:14; 18:8-9; 19:16-17; 29; 25:46). Therefore, we might reasonably think that John's primary concern is to assure those who believe in Yeshua of their future destinies. However, close attention to John's usage makes clear that this is not the case. In John "eternal life" is received now, in *this* world. It is a present possession, not merely anticipated in the future ... Eternal life is not merely Yeshua's gift to us – it is his presence among us and within us. This is why we need to "believe in" Yeshua in order to have that life – since "believing" means coming to him, loving him, remaining with him. When we draw near to Yeshua, we are drawing near to life. ... This identification of Yeshua with "life" in John is linked to Yeshua's deity ... To draw near to Yeshua is to draw near to God, and to draw near to God is to have life: "And this is eternal life, that they may know you, the only true God, and Yeshua the Messiah whom you have sent" (John 17:3).[23]

This understanding is also supported by N.T. Wright, who comments further:

> Unfortunately, the word for 'age' has often been translated as 'eternal' or 'eternity,' which has given modern readers the idea that John, and other early Christian writers who refer to God's new age, were thinking of something 'eternal' in the sense of 'purely spiritual,' something that had nothing to do with the world of space, time and matter. That's what people often hear when they read the phrase 'eternal life,' which is what most

---

23. Ibid., 147-148

translations have at verse 2. But this is mistaken. John, like Paul, and indeed like Jesus himself, is thinking of the new, the age to come, which God has promised. This is the future, and it really does work.

And God has provided an advance display of this future! ... The future had burst into the present, even though the present time wasn't ready for it. The word for that future is Life, life as it was meant to be, life in its full, vibrant meaning ... Of course, the very idea of God's new life becoming a person and stepping forward out of the future into the present is so enormous, so breathtaking ... Yes, repeats John: we heard, saw and touched this from-the-beginning Life. We knew him. We were his friends.[24]

Authorty and Eyewitnesses

In the opening prologue of 1 John the author encourages his audience, and counters the false teachers, by highlighting his authority as an apostle – as a direct eyewitness who personally knew Yeshua, and to whom authority was directly given. As Karen H. Jobes confirms, "These letters insist that this apostolic testimony [surpasses] any reinterpretation of Jesus by those who were not commissioned by him or who were far removed from personal knowledge of him."[25]

The reason John's instruction can be trusted is because he had a first-hand account of Yeshua and his teachings. He was also directly commissioned by the Messiah himself to spread this teaching to the rest of Israel and the world:

---

24. N.T. Wright, *The Early Christian Letters for Everyone* (New Testament for Everyone, Louisville: Westminster John Knox, 2011), 130-131.
25. Jobes, *op. cit.,* 23.

Matthew 28:18-20

---

18 Yeshua came and talked with them. He said, "All authority in heaven and on earth has been given to me. **19** Therefore, go and make people from all nations into talmidim, immersing them into the reality of the Father, the Son and the Ruach HaKodesh, **20** and teaching them to obey everything that I have commanded you. And remember! I will be with you always, yes, even until the end of the age."

Furthermore, not only was John and the other disciples personally commissioned to spread the message of Yeshua, they were also given the authority to do so:

Matthew 16:19

---

19 I will give you the keys of the Kingdom of Heaven. Whatever you prohibit on earth will be prohibited in heaven, and whatever you permit on earth will be permitted in heaven."

Matthew 18:18-20

---

18 Yes! I tell you people that whatever you prohibit on earth will be prohibited in heaven, and whatever you permit on earth will be permitted in heaven. **19** To repeat, I tell you that if two of you here on earth agree about anything people ask, it will be for them from my Father in heaven. **20** For wherever two or three are assembled in my name, I am there with them."

Most English translations use the terms "bind" and "loose" in both of these passages. However, the use of "prohibit" and "permit" (as used here) better convey the underlying concepts in a legal sense. People often mistakenly over-spiritualize these terms and use them to refer to authority in prayer or spiritual warfare. Although I do not deny that such spiritual authority is extended to Yeshua's followers, the direct context of the language is primarily halachic in nature.

According to David H. Stern, the terms "bind" and "loose" were used within first-century Judaism to mean "prohibit" and "permit" (the corresponding Hebrew is *"asar v'hittir"*).[26] Yeshua gave authority to his disciples to render halachic decisions, and similar language and imagery is used elsewhere within the New Testament.

In these opening verses to the Prologue of 1 John, the author establishes his authority to those who question it by reminding his audience that he was a direct witness to Yeshua and was directly given the authority to establish communal norms and practice (*halachah*).

He is also relating to his audience a truth which he will repeat over and over again in his letters, and which is a cornerstone of our theology, that Yeshua came in the flesh, and was experienced by his disciples as such (the reality of the incarnation). Notice the physical language he employs: *heard, seen, contemplated, touched, etc.* He is clearly telling his audience that he and the other disciples did not experience Yeshua metaphysically (as in a dream, vision or apparition), but tangibly. They ate with him, cried with him, traveled, and lived life with him. Because of the three years the disciples personally spent with Yeshua, John can confirm the reality of this truth.

This is the primary false teaching John seeks to counter and correct. However, he is also writing in a very positive way to encourage his audience in their faith, as he writes in verse 4, *"so that our joy may be complete."*

---

26. David H. Stern, *Jewish New Testament Commentary* (Clarksville: Jewish New Testament Publications, 1992), 56-58.

vv. 5-7 - Light And Darkness

5 And this is the message which we have heard from him and proclaim to you: God is light, and there is no darkness in him - none! **6** If we claim to have fellowship with him while we are walking in the darkness, we are lying and not living out the truth. **7** But if we are walking in the light, as he is in the light, then we have fellowship with each other, and the blood of his Son Yeshua purifies us from all sin.

Light and darkness were commonly employed themes within Early Judaism, especially in juxtaposition to each other. John regularly uses this imagery in his writings and is a common theme throughout 1 John. Herschel Shanks explains:

> The New Testament – particularly the Gospel of John – shares with the [Dead Sea Scrolls[27]] a dualistic theology which good and evil emanate from two different cosmic forces. History is thus a cosmic struggle between good (light) and evil (darkness). The so-called War Scroll from Qumran describes an apocalyptic battle between the Sons of Light and the Sons of Darkness. The Manual of Discipline admonishes: 'Love the Sons of Light. ... Hate all the Sons of Darkness. ... Love all that He has chosen and hate all He has rejected.[28]

In the Fourth Gospel Yeshua describes himself as "the light of the world; whoever follows me will not walk in darkness, but will have the light of life (John 8:12). John also employs light in reference

27. A collection of manuscripts discovered between 1946 and 1956 in caves around Khirbet Qumran. They are considered the most important archaeological discovery in relation to biblical studies and our understanding of the Second Temple period. For more on the Dead Sea Scrolls please refer to the Glossary.
28. Hershel Shanks, *The Mystery and Meaning of the Dead Sea Scrolls* (New York: Random House, 1998), 75-76.

to Yeshua in the Prologue (1:5) and 3:19-20, and in 12:35-36 the followers of Yeshua are referred to as "people of light." We also see this imagery used elsewhere in the New Testament, for example in the Gospel of Luke, in the parable of the unjust steward, Yeshua also speaks of the "sons of light" (Luke 16:8). And Paul employs similar language in 2 Corinthians 4:6 and Ephesians 5:7-14.[29]

Marianne Meye Thompson correctly notes that this imagery of light and darkness is drawn directly from the Tanakh:

> But we should also remember the Old Testament imagery to which John appeals. We can summarize the references to light in the Old Testament under three main headings. First, light attends and characterizes *God's self-manifestation* (Ex 3:1-6; 13:21-22; Ps 104:4). The psalmist pictures God clothed in garments of light (Ps 104:2; compare I Tim 6:16), an appropriate symbol for the One who is pure, righteous and holy. Second, *God's revelation* through the spoken and written word gives light. That word offers moral guidance and direction for living in accordance with God's will. Often quoted in this connection are verses from the Psalms: ''Thy word is a lamp to my feet and a light to my path'' (Ps 119:105, 130; 43:3; 56:13; Prov 6:23; Job 24:13; 29:3; Is 2:5; Dan 5:11, 14). Just as light shows people where to walk when it is dark, so God shows the way in which human beings are to walk: "in your light we see light" (Ps 36:9). Third, light symbolizes *God's salvation*. The psalmist celebrates God who is "my light and my salvation" (27:t;18:28), and light is a favorite image of the prophet Isaiah to depict God's saving activity on behalf of the people of God (9:1; 58:8, 10; 60:1, 19-20).[30]

---

29. Ibid., 76. The manual of Discipline is dated to c.100 B.C.E., whereas Luke is c.100 C.E. and John's writings are c.85-95 C.E.

30. Thompson, *op. cit.*, 41.

These images are, of course, related: as light shows the way in darkness, so also by virtue of God's revelation are we able to know God and the path in which we are to walk, a path that leads to God.[31] As Thompson further writes, "To have knowledge of God and to walk in the way that God requires constitutes salvation."[32]

As followers of Yeshua, we need to be those who walk in the light and live in truth, because when we do so, *"then we have fellowship with each other, and the blood of his Son Yeshua purifies us from all sin (v.7)."*

vv. 8-10 - Sin

---

8 If we claim not to have sin, we are deceiving ourselves, and the truth is not in us. **9** If we acknowledge our sins, then, since he is trustworthy and just, he will forgive them and purify us from all wrongdoing. **10** If we claim we have not been sinning, we are making him out to be a liar, and his Word is not in us.

No one can claim they are sinless. Otherwise, we are only deceiving ourselves. They is why we must acknowledge our sinful nature and do *Teshuva* (see below). For, if we confess our sins, *"he is trustworthy and just, he will forgive them and purify us from all wrongdoing (v.9)."*

John is concerned about sin because sin separates us from God. The Hebrew word *Chet* (חֵטְא), which is usually translated as "sin," better means to "miss the mark." It is to veer off-course from the path of proper spiritual, moral and ethical behavior.[33]

---

31. Ibid., 41-42.
32. Ibid., 42.
33. Wayne Dosick, *Living Judaism* (New York: Harper Collins, 1995), 139.

The reason sin separates us from God is because it causes us to go in the opposite direction of God's intention for our lives. Therefore, the answer to sin is *Teshuva* (תְּשׁוּבָה). Rabbi Jonathan Sacks notes, "There is no precise English translation of 'teshuva,' which means both 'return': homecoming, a physical act - and 'repentance': remorse, a change of heart and deed, a spiritual act. The reason the Hebrew word means both is because, for the Torah, sin leads to exile."[34]

According to Sacks, "Without repentance and forgiveness, the human condition would be unbearable."[35] However, our lives do not have to be unbearable. That is why we have Yeshua. Through Yeshua we are able to "return" and receive ultimate forgiveness and be restored to our Father in Heaven, and to a proper spiritual path.

---

34. Jonathan Sacks, *The Koren Rosh HaShanah Machzor* (Jerusalem: Koren Publishers, 2011), xix.
35. Ibid., xix.

Reflection Questions

1. What strikes you most about the Prologue?

2. What does John mean when he uses the term *the Word*?

3. Why did John write this book?

4. What does light represent in John's letter? And what does darkness represent?

5. What does it mean to "walk in the light"?

6. What is sin and why should we avoid it?

7. Is John's message still relevant today, and if so, why and how?

1 JOHN

CHAPTER 2

John's second chapter begins with a continuation of his dialogue from the first chapter. It focuses on having a correct relationship with God, which is defined by avoiding sin and remaining faithful to the commands of the Torah.

vv. 1-2 – Sin (Cont'd.)

---

1 My children, I am writing you these things so that you won't sin. But if anyone does sin, we have Yeshua the Messiah, the Tzaddik,[1] who pleads our cause with the Father. **2** Also, he is the kapparah for our sins - and not only for ours, but also for those of the whole world.

With these two verses John continues his discussion of sin (which began in 1:8).

My children – The term Children is used as both a general reference and as a way to refer to those who are not mature in their faith. Throughout the Tanakh the term is used regularly in reference to Israel, as well as other people groups (i.e., *Children of Israel*, etc.). According to Michelle Murray:

---

1. The Righteous One.

Jews are frequently referred to as God's children in the
Hebrew Bible (e.g., Deut. 14.1-2) and in rabbinic literature
(e.g., *m. Avot* 3.12). This imagery is used to convey the
special, intimate nature of the relationship between God and
the Jews – and how this special consecrated (or holy) status
places certain moral and behavioral expectations upon the
house of Israel ..."[2]

Philosophers and Jewish teachers also often used the term to
lovingly address their disciples. John extends this term "children"
to include all who follow Yeshua, regardless of whether they are
Jewish or not. Although this acknowledgement does not erase
all distinction and covenantal responsibilities between Jews and
Gentiles, in regard to faith and salvation it does equalize things
(see Eph. 2-3).

Tzaddik – Literally means "the righteous one." In Judaism
the concept is generally used to describe a godly, holy, righteous
individual. Within Chassidic and mystical traditions, such
individuals are thought to have special, supernatural powers,
and often attract many followers. These disciples often view the
Tzaddik as an intermediary between themselves and god. Therefore
they will devote their lives to following the *Tzaddik,* embodying
their teachings and directions, and raising up other disciples.

Who pleads our cause with the Father – Yeshua is an advocate
on our behalf before the Father (see also Heb. 7:25). He is a defense
attorney or intercessor pleading our case before the heavenly court.
As Keener notes, within the Tanakh, God pleads His people's case
before the nations (Jer. 50:34; 51:36) and in ancient Judaism we
find descriptions of God's mercy or Israel's merit pleading Israel's

---

2. Murray, *op. cit.,* 451.

case before God. Yeshua is naturally our advocate because of his position, his righteousness and his work (v.2).[3]

He is our kapparah – The Hebrew word *kapparah* (כפרה) means "atonement" or a reference to the atoning sacrifice. John is intentionally using the language of Yom Kippur – the Day of Atonement, the holiest day of the year. Only once a year the High Priest would enter the holiest place in the Temple (the *holy of holies*) after much preparation, purification, and sacrifices, and intercede before God on behalf of the people.[4]

According to John, Yeshua's sacrificial death provides both atonement and the remission of sins. What's the difference? Most people often conflate these two terms. However, each term, although related, also carry their own nuance. To understand this nuance we need to recognize the imagery of Yom Kippur which John is intentionally utilizing. Leviticus 16 describes the two goats used during the special *Avodah* service on Yom Kippur. Lots were cast by the High Priest to determine the fate of each goat. One served as a sin offering and the other "for making atonement." Each goat served a distinct role. The sin offering was directly on behalf of the sins of the people, whereas the atonement sacrifice brought Israel back into proper relationship with God. Therefore, what John is saying (by using this language and imagery of Yom Kippur), is that Yeshua's "atoning sacrifice" both covers our sins **and** reestablishes a correct relationship between us and God. It accomplishes both in a single act.

And not only for our [sins], but also for those of the whole world. – John is confirming that Yeshua's atonement is not only for Israel alone, but for the whole world. As N.T. Wright notes:

---

3. Keener, *op. cit.,* 738.
4. Leviticus 16; Mishnah, *Yoma* 4; etc.

It seems John is writing to Jewish [believers] who might have been tempted to suppose that Jesus, as Israel's Messiah, was the remedy for their problems, for their sins, and for them alone. Not a bit of it, says John. Jesus' sacrifice atones for our sins, 'and not ours only, but those of the whole world.'[5]

vv. 3-11 – Covenantal Responsibility

3 The way we can be sure we know him is if we are obeying his commands. 4 Anyone who says, "I know him," but isn't obeying his commands is a liar - the truth is not in him. 5 But if someone keeps doing what he says, then truly love for God has been brought to its goal in him. This is how we are sure that we are united with him. 6 A person who claims to be continuing in union with him ought to conduct his life the way he did. 7 Dear friends, I am not writing you a new command. On the contrary, it is an old command, which you have had from the beginning; the old command is the message which you have heard before. 8 Yet I am writing you a new command, and its reality is seen both in him and in you, because the darkness is passing away and the true light is already shining. 9 Anyone who claims to be in this light while hating his brother is still in the dark. 10 The person who keeps loving his brother remains in the light, and there is nothing in him that could make him trip. 11 But the person who hates his brother is in the dark - yes, he is walking in the dark, and he doesn't know where he is going, because the darkness has blinded his eyes.

John begins this next section (in verse 3) by telling us how we can be assured that we are in a correct relationship with Yeshua: By

---

5. Wright, *The Early Christian Letters for Everyone, op. cit.,* 137.

following his commands! If we are living in covenantal obedience then we can discern that we actually know him.

Obedience And Intimacy (vv. 3-6)

Verses 3-6 contrast the lifestyles of those who know God with those who do not, and connects intimacy (*knowing of Him*) with covenantal obedience (*observing the commands*). According to David H. Stern:

> In the *Tanakh* the word "know" can mean "have intimate experience"; here "knowing Yeshua" means having intimate spiritual experience with him, to the degree that one obeys his commands from the heart. Anything less is not true knowledge; there is a difference between giving mental assent to Yeshua's Messiahship and knowing him. Elsewhere Yochanan reports that Yeshua said, "If you love me, you will keep my commands," and "If you keep my commands you abide in my love" [John 14:15; 15:10; compare John 14:21; 15:14].[6]

We will also see this language of spiritual maturity used again in the poem below (vv.12-14), contrasting the wisdom of our ancestors with those who are younger (less mature) in their experience and faith.

Martin Buber relates a great Chassidic[7] teaching on spiritual maturity by exploring two types of faith:

> Why do we say [when we pray]: "Our God and the God of our fathers"?
>
> There are two kinds of people who believe in God. One believes because he has taken over the faith of his fathers,

---

6. Stern, *op. cit.,* 770.
7. For an explanation of this term, refer to the Glossary.

and his faith is strong. The other arrived has arrived at faith through thinking and studying. The difference between them is this: The advantage of the first is that, no matter arguments may be brought against it, his faith cannot be shaken; his faith is firm because it was taken over from his fathers. But there is one flaw in it: he has faith only in response to the command of man, and he has acquired it without studying and thinking for himself. The advantage of the second is that, because he found God through much thinking, he has arrived at a faith of his own. But here too there is a flaw: it is easy to shake his faith by refuting it through evidence. But he who unites both kinds of faith is invincible. And so we say, "Our God" with reference to our studies, and "God of our fathers" with an eye to tradition.[8]

John wants his audience to have a similar kind of faith, one that is solid, rooted in the Torah, and the history and experience of Israel, as understood through Yeshua's life and teachings, and as reliably passed on by the original apostles.

Regarding why observance is important to a healthy spiritual life, Marianne Meye Thompson notes:

And where there is no call for obedience, then all things are tolerated. "Do your own thing" becomes the motto. And so nothing can be labeled as "sinful." No act is clearly in the wrong. Thus, there is no need of forgiveness. But because John insists that God calls us to obey the commands that have been given, he also reminds us that when we fall short of keeping them, there is forgiveness in Christ.[9]

---

8. Martin Buber, *Ten Rungs: Hasidic Sayings* (New York: Schocken Books, 1973), 13.
9. Thompson, *op. cit.,* 51.

A New Command (v. 7)

How *"new"* is "new"? And how can something be both *"old ... from the beginning"* and *"new"*?

The commandment John mentions here is an "old law" (i.e., *"from the beginning"*) because it is from the Torah *(love your neighbor as yourself* - Lev. 19:18), however Yeshua's regular emphasis gave it further importance (see especially Matthew 22:36-40 and John 13:34-35).

John's use of both "old" and "new" implies both consistency and an expanded understanding. This is supported by the Messianic Jewish luminary, Paul Philip Levertoff, as well: "[T]he Messianic Age will bring not merely a revelation of the hidden meaning of the *old* Law, but a *new* revelation [italics his]."[10]

Often these passages are read through a supersessionist lens, as confirmation that what is described here replaces the Torah and Mosaic way of life. But that is not what John is communicating. What he is clearly saying is that these commands are the commands you already know (i.e., from the Torah). However, what John is providing is a new way of interpreting and applying them, as N.T. Wright explains:

> In Israel: this, he says, is actually the 'old command' which they had from the beginning. It isn't, in that sense, 'new.' If Moses had heard Jesus talk about love, he would have said, 'That's it! That's the heart of what these commandments were all about.' But, as John has already said in the letter (A plus B and now C), this command is also 'new' in a particular sense, because it is coming into the present, with Jesus himself, as a

---

10. Paul Philip Levertoff, *Love and the Messianic Age* (Marshfield: Vine of David, 2009), 47. Originally published in England in 1923.

gift from God's future. Love is the word that best describes the life of God's New Age, and we get to taste it and practice it in the present time.[11]

Over and over again John explains in different ways how Yeshua's "new command" is a continuation and expansion of what was previously given. This is evident in in the language he continually employs: *"not a new command but an old one," "which you have had from the beginning," etc.* He is assuring his audience that he is not teaching something that is a break with what was previously revealed, but a continuation and expansion of it.

This is important, especially for his Jewish audience and those who were God-fearers.[12] If what John is teaching is in fact a break with the Torah than it would be confirmation that John's teachings are in error and that Yeshua is not the Messiah. After all, Yeshua is first and foremost the Messiah of Israel, the *Word made flesh* (i.e., the Living Torah), and therefore also the vehicle of salvation extended to the Nations as well (Luke 2, Eph. 2-3, etc.). By definition, a Messiah who does not uphold the Torah is not the Messiah, pure and simple.[13]

Light And Darkness (vv. 8-11)

John again uses the duality of Light and Darkness (common Jewish themes within the Second Temple period). For more on this, see the commentary to 1 John 1:5-7.

---

11. Wright, *The Early Christian Letters for Everyone, op. cit.,* 141-142.
12. For more on the God-fearers please consult the Introduction, specifically the section on the Intended Recipients.
13. Matthew 5:17-20; etc.

Loving God and One Another (vv. 9-11)

By instructing us to walk in light by loving one another, John is re-packaging Yeshua's language condensing all of the Torah into two basic principles: Loving God and loving one another. This connection of love with observance is found directly in the Torah itself. Therefore, to understand the Bible's use of the word love, we need to understand the context in which it is regularly used. In the Bible, love is covenantal language. It is more than a feeling, it is a commitment.

Matthew 22:35-40

---

35 And one of them who was a Torah expert asked a *sh'eilah*[14] to trap him: **36** "Rabbi, which of the mitzvot in the Torah is the most important?" **37** He told him, "'You are to love ADONAI your God with all your heart and with all your soul and with all your strength.' **38** This is the greatest and most important mitzvah. **39** And a second is similar to it, 'You are to love your neighbor as yourself.' **40** All of the Torah and the Prophets are dependent on these two mitzvot."[15]

John's "new command" is really an expansion of Yeshua's teaching regarding "loving your neighbor as yourself."[16]

It has long been understood that all 613 commandments in the Torah are embodied in the 10 Commandments,[17] and that all 10 can be reduced into the very first: *"I am ADONAI your God who brought you out of the land of Egypt ... (Ex. 20:2)."*[18] The

---

14. A question; especially in a halachic sense.
15. A similar account is related in Mark 12:28-34.
16. Matthew 7:12; also see in the Talmud, *b. Shabbat* 31a.
17. Exodus 20.
18. According to the common Jewish reckoning of the 10 Commandments *(Aseret Dibrot).*

two tablets each represent two different types of commands. On the first tablet, the first five commandments fall in the category *mitzvot bein adam le-makom* (commandments between ourselves and God). The second tablet, and the next five commandments, fall into the category *mitzvot bein adam le-chavero* (commandments between a person and another person). [19] Therefore, when Yeshua boils everything down to "loving God" and "loving one another" he is essentially following a common summary of the 10 Commandments themselves (summarizing the tablets themselves), which again, represent all the commands in the Torah.

In the context of 1 and 2 John, "loving one another" includes hospitality extended to others, especially traveling emissaries, and cleaving to the community (rather than leaving it, as the secessionists were doing).[20]

For more on "Love and Observance" also see the commentary to 2 John 4-6.

vv. 12-14 - Instruction Poem

---

12 You children, I am writing you
   because your sins have been forgiven for his sake.
13 You fathers, I am writing you
   because you have known him who has existed   from
the beginning.
You young people, I am writing you
   because you have overcome the Evil One.
14 You children, I have written you
   because you have known the Father.

---

19. Harvey J. Fields, *A Torah Commentary for Our Times: Vol. III* (New York: UAHC Press, 1993), 53.
20. Keener, *op. cit.,* 749.

You fathers, I have written you
> because you have known him who has existed from
> the beginning.

You young people, I have written you
> because you are strong –
> the Word of God remains in you,
> and you have overcome the Evil One.

This poem serves a two-fold purpose – it is an affirmation of continuity regarding the previous section on covenantal faithfulness and responsibility, and serves as a transition into the next section on spiritual priorities.

John is again connecting and contrasting Yeshua's teachings with the sagely wisdom of our ancestors and tradition. John's teachings are meant to be understood within a context of continuity rather than a break with Judaism. This highly rhetorical poem also provides lessons in spiritual maturity as John describes his readers using three different categories: *children*, *young people*, and *fathers*. [21]

These categories describe a series of maturation and highlight stages of spiritual life:[22]

- Confession and forgiveness of sin

- Knowledge of the Father and the Son

- The indwelling of God's Word

- And victory over the Evil One

All of these are necessary for "walking in the light."

---

21. Jobes, *op. cit.,* 100-101.
22. Ibid., 101.

vv. 15-17 – Avoiding Sin

15 Do not love the world or the things of the world. If someone loves the world, then love for the Father is not in him; **16** because all the things of the world - the desires of the old nature, the desires of the eyes, and the pretensions of life - are not from the Father but from the world. **17** And the world is passing away, along with its desires. But whoever does God's will remains forever.

In this short section John emphasizes spiritual priorities because he is concerned about the effect of sin on the entire community. The reason is that that sin separates us from God. This is why we are to be set apart and not like the world around us (in relation to sin). This was an especially important message to these congregations now spread throughout the diaspora (within pagan societies with very different social and moral norms).

The desires of the old nature, the desires of the eyes, and the pretensions of life - Regarding verse 16, Keener comments:

The Old Testament often related the eyes to desire, especially sexual desire, and pride. Both Judaism and the philosophers (e.g., Aristotle, Epictetus,) condemned arrogant boastfulness. By listing the three vices together, John might allude, as some commentators have suggested, to Genesis 3:6, although the language here is more general.[23]

By pursuing a holy life, and staying focused on the truth, believers will "remain with God" and not be deceived by false teaching.

---

23. Keener, *op. cit.,* 739.

vv. 18-19 – The "Last Hour" And Fasle Teachers

18 Children, this is the Last Hour. You have heard that an Anti-Messiah is coming; and in fact, many anti-Messiahs have arisen now - which is how we know that this is the Last Hour. **19** They went out from us, but they weren't part of us; for had they been part of us, they would have remained with us.

John (as did many of the earliest believers) taught that they were in the final times before Messiah's return.

Anti-Messiahs – John directs this term against the False Teachers who were once a part of the community and broke away. He claims they were never true believers, otherwise they would still be united with the community (and in submission to the apostolic authority he appeals to in Chapter 1). Michelle Murray elaborates on the term "anti-christ/anti-messiah" and its origins:

> [T]his term is found in the NT only in these two letters (also 2.22; 4.3) and 2 Jn 7. The noun "christos" means "anointed one" or "messiah"; the prefix "anti-" can mean either "against" or "in place of." The antichrist is the adversary of God and Christ that comes in the end times. Antecedents to this idea can be found in Jewish literature and other sources (e.g., Dan 7.19-27; 8.9-11, 23-25; CD 8.2; 1QM 17.5-8; 11QMelch 2.12-13; and Sib. Or. 3.77-92, 6.11-15). In 1 John the sign of the (or an) antichrist seems to be false teaching, the denial of Jesus' messiahship, and the denial of the relation between God the Father and the Son.[24]

---

24. Murray, *op. cit.*, 450-451.

vv. 20-25 – Righteous Living

---

20 But you have received the Messiah's anointing from HaKadosh,[25] and you know all this. **21** It is not because you don't know the truth that I have written to you, but because you do know it, and because no lie has its origin in the truth. **22** Who is a liar at all, if not the person who denies that Yeshua is the Messiah? Such a person is an anti-Messiah - he is denying the Father and the Son. **23** Everyone who denies the Son is also without the Father, but the person who acknowledges the Son has the Father as well. **24** Let what you heard from the beginning remain in you. If what you heard from the beginning remains in you, you will also remain in union with both the Son and the Father. **25** And this is what he has promised us: eternal life.

John is encouraging his readers to remain true to the correct teaching they have received from him and other reliable teachers, and not be lured away by the false teachings of this break-away group.

This section also gives a little bit of a glimpse into what the false teachers were teaching: a denial of Yeshua's Messiahship and deity. However, those who remain faithful will receive their ultimate reward: Eternal Life!

Anointing from HaKadosh (the Holy One) – Murray points out that "anointing (marking with oil) is an indication of the beginning of a new task or taking on a new situation; the one who has marked the members of the community is the Spirit."[26]

---

25. The Holy One.
26. Murray, *op. cit.,* 451.

68

Everyone who denies the Son is also without the Father ... Stern rightly notes: "This passage invites comparisons with Yeshua's own statements – 'If you knew me you would know my Father too' (Yn 8:19), 'I and the Father are one' (Yn 10:30), and 'I am the Way – and the Truth and the Life; no one comes to the Father except through me' (Yn 14:6).[27]

How we live in this world is so important because it can provide a foretaste of what is to come. As Mark S. Kinzer explains:

> In the Hasidic worldview, Israel participates in the divine drama leading to redemption by living within the profane world in such a way as to lift it to the level of holiness. Kedushah is an eschatological reality, and Israel shares in that reality in anticipation and also extends that reality as part of the process of preparing for the final redemption. ... Israel waits for her redemption, but she also experiences now a foretaste of what she waits for.[28]

vv. 26-27 – Another Warning Against False Teaching

26 I have written you these things about the people who are trying to deceive you. **27** As for you, the Messianic anointing you received from the Father remains in you, so that you have no need for anyone to teach you. On the contrary, as his Messianic anointing continues to teach you about all things, and is true, not a counterfeit, so, just as he taught you, remain united with him.

You have no need for anyone to teach you - This section is not to be understood as being against proper instruction and leadership,

---

27. Stern, *op. cit.,* 772.
28. Kinzer, *Israel's Messiah and the People of God, op. cit.,* 102

but rather, an encouragement to not be lead astray by false teachers – those who claim to have a different teaching from what has already been proclaimed in previous verses. This is why, as we will see later in Chapter 4, we are to "test the Spirits," meaning, we are responsible for what we are being taught and who we are receiving guidance from. We need to be able to discern and rightly divide the truth (2 Tim. 2:15). John uses harsh language for the specific false teachers he is addressing by saying their deception is intentional: *"people who are trying to deceive you* (v.26).*"*

Stern points out, "Both *'you's'* are plural and refer to the believing community as a whole; there is no ground here for hyper-individualistic understanding of the Gospel wherein the views of other believers and the gathering of believers together are considered important."[29]

N.T. Wright elaborates:

> The true follower of Jesus the Messiah has been anointed by his Holy Spirit (vv. 20-21, 26-27) so that a real change of heart and character has happened. One of the key symptoms of that change is the recognition that Jesus is indeed the Messiah. He truly is the Son of God. The antimessianic movements are bound to deny this ... The greatest lie of all is to deny the Father and the Son (v.22). To deny that Jesus really is God's son is to cut off access to the Father as well, since we truly know the Father only through the Son. Don't do it, says John. These people are deceiving you (v.26). You know this deep down, because that "anointing" remains within you. Without anyone teaching you from the outside, you know the truth deep within.[30]

---

29. Ibid., 772.
30. Wright, *The Early Christian Letters for Everyone, op. cit.,* 22.

vv. 28-29 – Encouragemt to Remain Faithful

---

28 And now, children, remain united with him; so that when he appears, we may have confidence and not shrink back from him in shame at his coming. **29** If you know that he is righteous, you should also know that he is the Father of everyone who does what is right.

In these two transitional verses, John encourages his readers and listeners to remain faithful and not lose hope, but to stay strong and live righteously. We also again see John's loving, pastoral reference to his readers as "children."

Children, remain united with him - Marianne Meye Thompson reassures:

> These various commands, which urge continued steadfastness, are not intended to frighten the readers or to suggest their inadequacies or failures to abide in Christ. Quite the contrary, those words encourage them to *continue* faithfully in the direction that they have been heading all along. The command admonishes them, but it does so by affirming them in their present course. They have abided; they must continue to do so. Encouragement and exhortation are joined together.[31]

We may have confidence and not shrink back from him in shame - Craig S. Keener notes, "In Jewish tradition, the coming of God to judge the world would be a fearful day for those who were disobedient to his will (cf. Amos 5:18-20)."[32] However, as his children we can have confidence because we are united with Yeshua.

---

31. Thompson, *op. cit.,* 85.
32. Keener, *op. cit.,* 741.

The language of verse 29 literally reads, *"... everyone who lives righteously has been born of him* (πᾶς ὁ ποιῶν τὴν δικαιοσύνην ἐξ αὐτοῦ γεγέννηται).*"* Stern's translation above communicates this idea but does not quite capture the emphasis on new birth (i.e., *"been born of him"*). Jobes points out, "this is the first occurrence in the letter of the theme of new birth with God as Father, a theme that is foundational in John's gospel (1:3; 3:3-8) and now becomes a persistent and important theme in this letter as well (1 John 3:9; 4:7; 5:1, 4, 18)."[33] She goes on to note, "The new birth metaphor is found also in the apostle Peter's writings (1 Pet 1:3), where it explains the radical transformation necessary to enter the kingdom of God."[34]

Reflection Questions

1. Why does John use language from Yom Kippur in addressing sin and forgiveness?

2. Why does John connect love with covenantal obedience?

3. What does it specifically mean to "love God"? And what does it mean to "love others"?

4. How do we avoid false teaching? And how can we discern correct teaching?

5. What does it mean to *"be born of him"* (v.29)? Why is spiritual rebirth important?

---

33. Jobes, *op. cit.,* 140.
34. Ibid., 140.

1 JOHN

CHAPTER 3

This chapter focuses on behaving as children of God – basically, how we should conduct our lives because of our relationship with God through Yeshua.

vv. 1-2 – We Are God's Children

---

1 See what love the Father has lavished on us in letting us be called God's children! For that is what we are. The reason the world does not know us is that it has not known him. **2** Dear friends, we are God's children now; and it has not yet been made clear what we will become. We do know that when he appears, we will be like him; because we will see him as he really is.

This section begins back in v.29 with the last verse of the previous chapter.

Letting us be called God's children - "Children" is used as a both a general reference, and as a way to refer to those who are not mature in their faith. We see throughout the Tanakh (e.g. Deut. 14:1-2) and early rabbinic literature (e.g., *m. Avot* 3.12), that the Jewish people are frequently referred to as God's children. According to Michele Murray: "This imagery is used to convey the special, intimate nature of the relationship between God and the Jews – and how this special consecrated (or holy) status places certain moral and behavioral expectations upon the house of Israel ..."[1]

Acts 15 describes, and Paul elaborates on in Ephesians 2-3, a similar relationship that has now been extended to those Gentiles who have put their *faith-trust* in Yeshua. As a result, Gentiles not only share in the blessings along with the Jewish people, but also similar moral and behavioral expectations (although not the same covenantal observance requirements).

Philosophers and Jewish teachers also often used the term "children" to lovingly address their disciples.

Karen H. Jobes points out: "John is still concerned with the topic of God's children living righteously, but he now brings love back into discussion again. Because God is eternal, his children have eternal life. Because God is righteous, his children [must] live righteously. Because God loves, his children must love (3:10)."[2]

We are God's children now – According to John, we, as God's children, are a work in progress. This is suggested by the emphatic fronting of "now" (νῦν). We are *now* children of the Father, even with all our faults and flaws, and, yes, sins. "But it is not God's purpose to allow his children to be as we are now, for the full benefit of our status cannot be even imagined in this world (cf. 1 Cor. 2:9)."[3]

Marianne Meye Thompson highlights:

> The kind of love God demonstrates is active and creative love, which "calls" us the children of God. "Calling" means more

---

1. Murray, *op. cit.*, 451.
2. Jobes, *op. cit.*, 141.
3. Ibid., 141.

than naming. It means the inauguration of a relationship, of a reality that can best be pictured by the metaphor of being God's own children. By God's creative act of love, we belong to God as surely and permanently as children belong to their parents. The Elder emphasizes this new relationship when he writes, *And that is what we are!* and *now we are children of God*. We do not simply *look at* a love that is external to us and marvel at its greatness; we *know* a love that resides within us [emphases hers].[4]

We do know that when he appears, we will be like him – As Jobes rightfully notes:

John can say with confidence that when Jesus returns, "we will be like him." Jesus himself said, "Because I live, you also will live" (John 14:19). Because Jesus shared in our humanity fully, whatever he became as a resurrected human being, we also will become. But John's concern here is not about a metaphysical speculation on the afterlife; it is about ethical living and reflecting the character of the Father. It is about the children bearing a family resemblance to the Father."[5]

Rabbi Yechiel Tzvi Lichtenstein[6] comments on this verse:

Isaiah 5:28 says, 'For they shall see eye to eye when the Lord shall bring again Zion.' On this basis John proved here that *'when he appears, we will be like him.'* The proof that we will see him is that since in the flesh it is impossible to see God – as it is written, 'Man shall not see me and live' (Exodus 33:20) – so it must be that *'we will be like him'* means that

---

4. Thompson, *op. cit.,* 88.
5. Jobes, *op. cit.,* 142.
6. A great 19th century Jewish believer who published a monumental commentary in Hebrew on the New Testament, published in consecutive volumes between 1891-1904 in Leipzig, Germany.

we will be comparable with him. And this is so, for we will have a spiritual body like his – as Paul said in Philippians 3:21, 'He will change the bodies we have in this humble state and make them like his glorious body.' Likewise the sages cited in *Mivchar HaPninim* ('The Choice Pearls') said, 'If I knew, I would be,' that is, 'If I knew God, I would already be like him.'[7]

vv. 3-6 – Purity Against Sin

3 And everyone who has this hope in him continues purifying himself, since God is pure. 4 Everyone who keeps sinning is violating Torah - indeed, sin is violation of Torah. 5 You know that he appeared in order to take away sins, and that there is no sin in him. 6 So no one who remains united with him continues sinning; everyone who does continue sinning has neither seen him nor known him.

Hope – The Greek word translated as "hope" in verse 3 (ἐλπίδα, *elpida*) has a stronger sense of certainty than the English word does.[8] As Jobes emphasizes:

> But when John speaks of the [believer's] eschatological future, there is no uncertainty because it is based on what Jesus Christ has *already* done. The only reason that this attitude is referred to as a "hope" is that it is still future. It is a certain hope that is merely awaited.[9]

Purifying himself, since God is pure - From a biblical perspective, purity (and specifically *ritual purity*), is necessary

---

7. As quoted in: Stern, *op. cit.*, 773.
8. Jobes, *op. cit.*, 142.
9. Ibid., 142.

for coming into contact with God (see Isa. 6:5-7; Mal. 3:2; etc.)[10] Therefore, it should not be too surprising that John uses language and imagery related to ritual purity (something that was central to a Temple-centered Judaism), however, he also adds a twist which we also see with James and Peter (James 4:8 and 1 Peter 1:22). John uses this language of ritual purity to refer to the moral transformation of the believer. Just as ritual purity set one apart for service unto God or to enter into His presence, so too all believers are to be set apart by a moral consecration in their way of life.[11]

Everyone who keeps sinning is violating Torah ... - Or, as rendered by some translations, "Everyone who does sin indeed is lawless, for sin is lawlessness." Since, as believers, we are to be more like Yeshua, we need to live like Yeshua in our behavior. Anytime we sin we act in a way that is not like Yeshua. Jobes notes that John here is pointing out the true nature of sin – "not as individual random acts, but as originating from an attitude that resents God's moral demands on their lives, an attitude that John refers to as "lawlessness" [or *"a violation of Torah,"* as Stern puts it].[12]

The specific word John uses here for "lawlessness" is ἀνομία *(anomia)*, which literally means "un-law," or in better English, "lawlessness." According to Jobes:

> When John says that sin is *anomia,* he is saying more than that every sin is in some sense an infraction of the Mosaic law ... To be "lawless" does not mean simply to break the law; it means to disdain the very idea of a law to which one must submit ... *Anomia* is the rejection of God's authority and the exaltation of the autonomy of the self.[13]

---

10. Murray, *op. cit.,* 451.
11. Jobes, *op. cit.,* 142-143.
12. Ibid., 143.
13. Ibid., 143.

So no one who remains united with him continues sinning - As N.T. Wright correctly emphasizes, "John is quite clear, and we can't get away from it. Following Jesus, 'abiding in him' (one of John's regular ways of saying 'belonging to him,' implying that kind of life-sharing we saw earlier) means a transformed character."[14]

John is clearly instructing his audience to be in submission to the ways of God. As Jobes stresses, "The foundation of a right relationship with God is acknowledging that He himself defines the standard of right and wrong, and that we must be willing to submit ourselves to His authority."[15]

vv. 7-10 – Warning Against Being Deceived

7 Children, don't let anyone deceive you - it is the person that keeps on doing what is right who is righteous, just as God is righteous. 8 The person who keeps on sinning is from the Adversary, because from the very beginning the Adversary has kept on sinning. It was for this very reason that the Son of God appeared, to destroy these doings of the Adversary. 9 No one who has God as his Father keeps on sinning, because the seed planted by God remains in him. That is, he cannot continue sinning, because he has God as his Father. 10 Here is how one can distinguish clearly between God's children and those of the Adversary: everyone who does not continue doing what is right is not from God. Likewise, anyone who fails to keep loving his brother is not from God.

---

14. Wright, *The Early Christian Letters for Everyone, op. cit.,* 151.
15. Jobes, *op. cit.,* 144.

John is again warning his audience against sin and being seduced by false teachings. According to Jobes:

> By addressing his readers once again as "children" (Τεκνία), John recalls to mind the question of whose children they are. The reference to the devil implies the question of whom they resemble, the Father or the evil one ... John fears his readers may be misled about the relationship between what one does and who one is. The one who does what is right according to God's standard and who, therefore, acknowledges and accepts God's authority is righteous in the same way as [Yeshua] was ... Any claim to be a child of God while living in ways that contradict God's revealed standards is a false claim.[16]

Jobes continues:

> To sin is to be like the devil because from the beginning, in Eden, the devil encouraged disobedience to God and, ironically, justified it as the way of being like God (Gen 3:5) ... Satan twisted the idea into the impulse to sin. Adam and Eve, and all human beings after them, grasped at becoming like God through rejecting God's authority over them. ... To persist in sin reveals the presence of *anomia* (3:4) and contradicts any claim to have been born of God.[17]

Furthermore, in verses 6 and 9, where it says that "No one who has God as his Father keeps on sinning," as David H. Stern notes, John "is not saying that once a person confesses faith in Yeshua he will never again commit sin; this is already clear from 1:5-2:2. On the contrary, his point is that a believer should never intend to sin."[18]

---

16. Ibid., 146.
17. Ibid., 146.
18. Stern, *op. cit.*, 773.

vv. 11-18 – Loving One Another (Love in Action)

11 For this is the message which you have heard from the beginning: that we should love each other 12 and not be like Cain, who was from the Evil One and murdered his own brother. Why did he murder him? Because his own actions were evil, and his brother's were righteous. 13 Don't be amazed, brothers, if the world hates you. 14 We, for our part, know that we have passed from death to life because we keep loving the brothers. The person who fails to keep on loving is still under the power of death. 15 Everyone who hates his brother is a murderer, and you know that no murderer has eternal life in him. 16 The way that we have come to know love is through his having laid down his life for us. And we ought to lay down our lives for the brothers! 17 If someone has worldly possessions and sees his brother in need, yet closes his heart against him, how can he be loving God? 18 Children, let us love not with words and talk, but with actions and in reality!

Having laid down his life – Because of Yeshua's sacrificial death on our behalf, we can know true love. Michelle Murray notes, "the rabbinic term 'Kiddush HaShem' denotes martyrdom, in particular, the willingness to die a martyr in order to sanctify ('kiddush') God's name ('ha-Shem'). Though the term is rabbinic, the concept is biblical, based on Lev. 22.32 ..."[19]

Paul Philip Levertoff, explains:

> God's love for His Son brings forth a corresponding love of the Son for Him. It expresses itself in the glorification, or sanctification, of God's Name by the Son. The highest motive

---

19. Murray, *op. cit.,* 452.

80

of Jewish piety, *Kiddush HaShem* ["sanctification of the Name"] is His supreme objective. When the Son summarizes the work that He has done on earth, He does not refer to any empirical success, such as the love and faith which He had awakened among men, but the service which He had rendered to God: "I have *glorified* Thee on earth" (John 17:4). He lives and dies for God's honor. His love is a conscious self-oblation to the will of God.[20]

John returns to his common theme of love for one another. The reason this is routinely emphasized by John, as Levertoff notes, is because, "The true test of love for Him is love for the brethren."[21] As a counterexample to loving one another, John gives the example of Cain, the first murderer. The reason, as Jobes points out, is "Cain's motive for killing his brother reveals a foundational spiritual principle about life in this world: those who do not do what is right hate those who do."[22] She goes on to state: "Because Cain was the first murderer in the biblical story of humankind, in later tradition he was known as the archetype sinner ... Cain is therefore the personification of *anomia*."[23]

Don't be amazed, brothers, if the world hates you. - The world, which is self-deceived, resents those who try to obey God through living according to biblical values and principles.[24] As difficult as it is, we need to be able to live righteously despite possible judgement and pressure from those around us, or from society.

This language is very similar to Yeshua's words as recorded in John's Gospel:

---

20. Levertoff, *op. cit.,* 74-75.
21. Ibid., 78.
22. Jobes, *op. cit.,* 155.
23. Ibid., 155.
24. Ibid., 155-156.

John 15:19-21

---

19 If you belonged to the world, the world would have loved its own. But because you do not belong to the world -- on the contrary, I have picked you out of the world -- therefore the world hates you. **20** Remember what I told you, `A slave is not greater than his master.' If they persecuted me, they will persecute you too; if they kept my word, they will keep yours too. **21** But they will do all this to you on my account, because they don't know the One who sent me.

The world – We need to be careful not to read warnings of *the world* as a reference to every possible thing that is a part of our life on earth. Rather, it specifically refers to influences that hinder our relationship with God. We were placed in this world to tend and take care of it, and to enjoy it (Gen. 2:15). We are also supposed to enjoy life and one another. However, we also need to be vigilant that life's influences do not control us. Being "in the world but not of this world" has to do with where our influences and enjoyment ultimate come from, and are dictated by.

Everyone who hates his brother is a murderer ... – John again makes the stunning association of hate with murder (again a reference to Cain). As Jobes notes: "In this context, everyone who hates their brother is like Cain, who hated his brother for living rightly before God."[25]

The association of hate with murder is embodied in the biblical notion of *"b'tzelem Elohim,"* that all people are created in the image of God (Gen. 1:27). And this association also comes directly from the way Jews have interpreted the Ten Commandments:

1.אנוכי ה' אלוהיך ...	6. לא תרצח
I am the Lord your God ...	You shall not murder

---

25. Ibid., 157.

These commands are the top commandment on each tablet. Visually, with the tablets side by side, the interpretation is clear … *"I am the Lord your God"* (and we are created in God's image) and *"You shall not murder."* Therefore, hate is directly linked with (and ultimately leads to) murder. Murder is not only an assault against another human being, but also an assault against God.

Within rabbinic tradition there are also many of these same connections. In fact, there is a discussion in the Mishnah that makes the same association with Cain:

Mishnah, Sanhedrin 4:5

שֶׁכֵּן מָצִינוּ בְקַיִן שֶׁהָרַג אֶת אָחִיו, שֶׁנֶּאֱמַר דְּמֵי אָחִיךָ צֹעֲקִים, אֵינוֹ אוֹמֵר דַּם אָחִיךָ אֶלָּא דְּמֵי אָחִיךָ, דָּמוֹ וְדַם זַרְעִיוֹתָיו. דָּבָר אַחֵר, דְּמֵי אָחִיךָ,

שֶׁהָיָה דָמוֹ מֻשְׁלָךְ עַל הָעֵצִים וְעַל הָאֲבָנִים. לְפִיכָךְ נִבְרָא אָדָם יְחִידִי, לְלַמֶּדְךָ, שֶׁכָּל הַמְאַבֵּד נֶפֶשׁ אַחַת, מַעֲלֶה עָלָיו הַכָּתוּב כְּאִלּוּ אִבֵּד עוֹלָם מָלֵא.
וְכָל הַמְקַיֵּם נֶפֶשׁ אַחַת, מַעֲלֶה עָלָיו הַכָּתוּב כְּאִלּוּ קִיֵּם עוֹלָם מָלֵא.

For so have we found it with Cain that murdered his brother, for it says, *"The blood of your brother cries out"* (Gen. 4:10). It doesn't say, "The blood of your brother", but rather "The bloods of your brother" meaning his blood and the blood of his descendants. Another saying is, "The bloods of your brother" that his blood was cast over trees and stones. Therefore, Adam [from whom all humanity descended] was created singly, to teach us that whoever destroys a single life is considered by Scripture to have destroyed the whole world, and whoever saves a single life is considered by Scripture to have saved the whole world.[26]

26. Translation mine, adapted from: Sefaria, accessed May 8, 2019 - https://www.sefaria.org/Mishnah_Sanhedrin.4.5?lang=bi&with=all&lang2=en

This is also why Yeshua taught in the Sermon on the Mount:

Matthew 5:21-22

> **21** "You have heard that our fathers were told, 'Do not murder,' and that anyone who commits murder will be subject to judgment. **22** But I tell you that anyone who nurses anger against his brother will be subject to judgment; that whoever calls his brother, `You good-for-nothing!' will be brought before the Sanhedrin; that whoever says, `Fool!' incurs the penalty of burning in the fire of *Gei-Hinnom!*

How we treat one another matters because it is a direct reflection of our true devotion to God. If we love God, we will love one another. And if we mistreat, and God forbid, even murder one another, than we cannot truly say way love God. We need to examine ourselves and measure our current spiritual health by the health of the relationships around us. The way we treat others (and our intolerances toward others) is an exact barometer measuring how close we really are to Yeshua. If we want to be true followers of him (and not just those who claim the title), we need to work on being more compassionate, caring, patient, and loving.

vv. 19-22 – Assurance of Our Faith

> **19** Here is how we will know that we are from the truth and will set our hearts at rest in his presence: **20** if our hearts know something against us, God is greater than our hearts, and he knows everything. **21** Dear friends, if our hearts know nothing against us, we have confidence in approaching God; **22** then, whatever we ask for, we receive from him; because we are obeying his commands and doing the things that please him.

John is encouraging his readers that they can have assurance of their good standing with God as long as they are faithful and live righteously. We are also taught that along with the assurance that we are living in the truth, we can *have confidence in approaching God*.

Set our hearts at rest – According to Michelle Murray:

> [T]he Hebrew Bible views the heart as the seat of the emotional and intellectual inner life of a human being; the Hebrew word for heart, 'lev(av),' was used metaphorically to refer to the source of the intellectual activities of a person (e.g., 1 Kings 8.48; Isa 10.7; Ezek 36.26). The laws of God were considered to have been written on the heart of humans (Ps 37.31). The rabbis also adopted the view that the heart was the seat of the emotions and intellect; most rabbinic references to the heart pertain to the sphere of ethics (e.g., *m. Avot* 2.9), and prayer is understood to be the "service of the heart" (*y. Ber.* 4.1; 7a).[27]

Whatever we ask for, we receive from him – This boldness results from our experience of the love of God.

But this can also be a difficult issue: when we ask, but we *don't* seem to receive. We all ask God at various times why He did not answer our prayers which we may have sought with true faith and confidence. However, it is not always that our prayers go unanswered, but rather, our prayers are not always answered in the way and timing we expect. And yet, there are indeed unanswered prayers. We can all look back and thank God that he did not answer certain prayers we may have prayed. Because they would have resulted in terrible decisions. We also need to consider whether

---

27. Murray, *op. cit.*, 452.

what we pray for was truly according to *God's* will (rather than ours). Furthermore, we must also recognize that those unanswered prayers are usually exceptions. Every single day we can, *and do*, witness results. Whether immediate or over time. When we pray, each time we must *have confidence in approaching God;* because we have assurance our prayers are heard and that we have spiritual authority as God's children.

vv. 23-24 – Unity In Observance

---

23 This is his command: that we are to trust in the person and power of his Son Yeshua the Messiah and to keep loving one another, just as he commanded us. **24** Those who obey his commands remain united with him and he with them. Here is how we know that he remains united with us: by the Spirit whom he gave us.

This is the concluding section, and closing verses, of Chapter 3.

This is his command - Faith in Yeshua and our love for one another are not optional points of piety. They are directly commanded by God and the fundamental building blocks upon which the rest of our spiritual lives are built.

Those who obey his commands remain united with him and he with them. - How can we be sure, even if we observe the *mitzvot*, we are in right standing with God? By His Spirit! Through the impartation of the Spirit into our lives, and spiritual fruit confirming spiritual transformation, we have confirmation that we have been redeemed, forgiven, and empowered for the work of the Kingdom. And each day that we witness God's Spirit moving within and through us is continual confirmation we remain united with Yeshua.

When lived out through the impartation of the Spirit, and in correct perspective through Yeshua and his teachings, the *mitzvot* provide 613 different ways to connect with our Creator. They are like rungs on a ladder, that each draw us closer to heaven and each other. Our observance matters. That's what John is directly saying. But what matters even more is our *kavanah*[28] and incorporation of the *mitzvot*, as understood in and through Yeshua. As Mark S. Kinzer inspires us:

> Messianic Judaism involves more than the subtle tweaking of an existing form of Jewish life and thought – adding a few elements required by faith in Yeshua and subtracting a few elements incompatible with that faith. Instead, the Judaism we have inherited – and continue to practice – is entirely bathed in the bright light of Yeshua's revelation. In a circular and dynamic interaction, our Judaism provides us with the framework required to interpret Yeshua's revelation even as it is reconfigured by that revelation. In this way our Judaism and our Yeshua-faith are organically and holistically 'integrated.'[29]

---

28. *Kavanah* (כונה) mean "intention." It is the focus, intention, or meaning through which our observance and prayer flow out.
29. Kinzer, *Israel's Messiah and the People of God, op. cit.,* 452.

Reflection Questions

1. Why do you think John continually chooses to refer to his readers/listeners as "children"?

2. Why is it so important to behave as "children of God"? Isn't it enough to just believe in God? Why should how we live matter?

3. According to John, what are ways we can measure spiritual maturity?

4. Do you struggle with assurance of your salvation through Yeshua? In John's letters, what does he describe as assurances of our redemption?

5. How does observance provide a vehicle for unity?

1 JOHN

CHAPTER 4

Chapter four opens with a discussion on testing what we are taught (*testing every spirit*). The rest of the chapter then continues with a more intense message on love, building on the discussion from chapters 2 and 3.

vv. 1-3 – Testing What We Are Taught

1 Dear friends, don't trust every spirit. On the contrary, test the spirits to see whether they are from God; because many false prophets have gone out into the world. **2** Here is how you recognize the Spirit of God: every spirit which acknowledges that Yeshua the Messiah came as a human being is from God, **3** and every spirit which does not acknowledge Yeshua is not from God - in fact, this is the spirit of the Anti-Messiah. You have heard that he is coming. Well, he's here now, in the world already!

In many circles and congregations, if someone claims to be a prophet, or gets up and gives a prophetic word, that's supposed to be the end of it … we're just supposed to accept that whatever is said is a direct word from God without testing it. However, claims of spiritual truth are one of the issues John addresses right away.

Don't trust every spirit. On the contrary, test the spirits – John's instruction refers not only to spiritual dynamics but also the motivation of individuals. On this idea, it is worth quoting Karen H. Jobes at length::

> One of the exegetical issues that needs attention here is how to understand the referent of "spirits" (πνεύματα), the only occurrence of the plural form in John's gospel and letters. The Greek word *pneuma* (πνεῦμα) has a large semantic range; it can be used to refer to physical wind (Matt 11:7; 14:30, 32), breath (Acts 17:25; 2 Thess 2:8), angels (Heb 1:7, 14), demons (Matt 8:16; 12:45), other noncorporeal beings (Num 27:16 LXX), the incorporeal part of the human person (2 Cor 7:1; Col 2:5), and the third member of the Trinity (Matt 28:19). Of these possible referents, demons are most often assumed to be the spirits mentioned here.
>
> But the meaning should be controlled by John's use of the same term in 3:24, where it was used to refer to the manifestation of God's Spirit in the life of a believer. This is consistent with Jesus' teaching in John's gospel (John 3:8) ... The usage is also consistent with Paul's teaching on the manifestations of the Spirit (1 Cor 14:12). This use of the word can be defined as "the Spirit of God's people or selected agents." Similarly the word *pneuma* can also refer to activating impulses that are not of God (2 Cor 11:4) but that are expressed in human words and actions, which is likely the sense to be understood here in 4:1. ... John wants his readers to recognize that ... there are other forces at work than the Holy Spirit, and he refers to those forces as "spirits" that must be tested. ... John's readers need to understand that not everything said or done by someone who professes to have the Holy Spirit is of God, because many false prophets have gone out into the world.[1]

---

1. Jobes, *op. cit.,* 176-177.

That is why we must learn to use discernment and to test everything. Over and over again in Scripture we are admonished to weigh what we are taught against what we know to be true. There are many examples of this, but two should suffice. The first is the familiar account of Paul's experience at the synagogue in Berea (Acts 17), where it says: *they eagerly welcomed the message, checking the Tanakh every day to see if the things Sha'ul was saying were true (v.11)."* It's important to note that *"they eagerly welcomed the message."* They were not skeptics or challenging Paul. However, even though they resonated with the message, they still checked *"the Tanakh every day to see if the things Sha'ul was saying were true."* And Paul does not reprimand them or get defensive, but praises them for it.

A second example is Paul's instruction in 1 Corinthians 14:29-33 regarding prophets speaking prophetic words: *"Let two or three prophets speak, while the others weigh what is said..."* Paul clearly states that whenever a prophetic word is given, even if from a reliable source, the word must be weighed by other prophets. This is the opposite of what often happens within modern-day circles. In many congregations and settings, if someone claims to be a prophet, or gets up and gives a prophetic word, that's supposed to be the end of it. We're just supposed to assume that whatever is said is a direct word from God without questioning or weighing it. However, according to John, we are supposed to test spirits and spiritual dynamics, and also test what is taught and spoken. As Jobes cautioned above, "not everything said or done by someone who professes to have the Holy Spirit is of God."

This concern for testing the words of a prophet go back to the Tanakh, where, for example, Deuteronomy 18:20-22 provides two criteria: "(1) true prophets speak only on behalf of the God of Israel alone (i.e., not on behalf of other gods), and (2) a true prophecy will come to pass."[2]

According to Craig S. Keeners:

> Judaism especially associated the Spirit of God with prophecy but acknowledged the existence of false prophets, who John says are the moved by other spirits. His readers would understand his point; Jewish people were familiar with the idea of other spirits beside the Spirit of God ... There were many pagan ecstatics in Asia Minor, as well as Jewish mystics claiming special revelations; the need for discernment would be acute.[3]

Michele Murray further comments:

> The rabbis likewise were concerned about the distinction between true and false prophets; they warned, for example, that false prophets would entice Jews to transgress Mosaic law by promising great rewards (e.g., *Pesiq. Rav Kah.* 24.15). Rabbis were particularly concerned about the relationship between prophecy and law, and which had more authority: "Until now [in the age of Alexander the Great] the prophets prophesied through the medium of the Holy Spirit; from now on, incline your ear and hearken to the words of the sages" (*Seder Olam Rab.* 30).[4]

Because many false prophets have gone out into the world - John's concern is directed toward the false teachers who were teaching people something contrary to what was taught by the apostles. Therefore, John writes that the way to know whether they are really

---

2. Murray, *op. cit.,* 453.
3. Keener, *op. cit.,* 743.
4. Murray, *op. cit.,* 453.

from God is to test them. As Paul also writes in 1 Thessalonians 5:21: *"But do test everything – hold on to what is good."*

And how do we test these teachings and/or "spirits"? John gives us the answer: *"Every spirit which acknowledges that Yeshua the Messiah came as a human being is from God; and every spirit which does not acknowledge Yeshua is not from God – in fact, this is the spirit of the Anti-Messiah (v.3)."*

The author uses the term "anti-Messiah" in verse 3 as a neologism (see also 1 John 2:18 and 2 John 7) to indicate that the opponents are literally "against the Messiah," rather than a reference to a specific satanic agent.[5]

You have heard that he is coming - When John speaks of Yeshua's "coming into the world," it is important to note that he is not just speaking of his visible appearance, but rather his coming as a salvific act. Yeshua's mission by coming into the world was a salvific mission. Therefore, as Jobes emphasizes, when we confess that Yeshua "has come" in the flesh, it "does not simply mean that Jesus was a historical person, but expresses the redeeming significance of his incarnate life, death, and resurrection on behalf of the human race."[6]

Jobes goes on to note, "The understanding that Jesus Christ, the Son of God, became a human being to reveal God the Father is at the heart of John's orthodoxy."[7] This was a Christological dispute. And although, as we've noted elsewhere, it has been common to read these verses against the backdrop of Docetism (Yeshua only *appeared* to be human), there are also "several other kinds of heretical views that this statement refutes."[8]

---

5. Galumbush, *op. cit.,* 457.
6. Jobes, *op. cit.,* 178.
7. Ibid., 179.
8. Ibid., 179.

v. 4-6 – Encouragement

4 You, children, are from God and have overcome the false prophets, because he who is in you is greater than he who is in the world. 5 They are from the world; therefore, they speak from the world's viewpoint; and the world listens to them. 6 We are from God. Whoever knows God listens to us; whoever is not from God doesn't listen to us. This is how we distinguish the Spirit of truth from the spirit of error.

You, children, are from God – John again uses the term "children" as a both a general reference, and as a way to refer to those who are not yet mature in their faith. John encourages his audience that they are able to overcome these errant teachings because the power of God within them is greater than the spiritual forces behind the False Teachers.

Keener adds, "The Dead Sea Scrolls similarly distinguish between God's children and the rest of the world, though they go far beyond John in asserting that every act is determined be either the spirit of truth or the spirit of error."[9]

vv. 7-10 – Love is From God

7 Beloved friends, let us love one another; because love is from God; and everyone who loves has God as his Father and knows God. 8 Those who do not love, do not know God; because God is love. 9 Here is how God showed his love among us: God sent his only Son into the world, so that through him we might have life. 10 Here is what love is: not that we have loved God, but that he loved us and sent his Son to be the kapparah for our sins.

---

9. Keener, *op. cit.,* 743.

In this next section (7-16), John redirects his focus back to love, and particularly "identifies both the source and definition of love as God himself. God's love is most supremely expressed in the sending of [His] Son as an atoning sacrifice for our sin so that we might live eternally through him."[10] As Jobes further comments, "The rationale for the love command is that love is a defining characteristic of God. Therefore, those who have been born of God are also defined by their love for others."[11]

Beloved friends – The Elder again refers to his audience as *agapetoi* (beloved, ἀγαπητοὶ), reminding them they are loved, not only by the author, but by God.[12]

Those who do not love, do not know God – This is again a return to the command to love one another, an extension of the discussion from Chapters 2 and 3 (see specifically the commentary to 2:9-22 and 3:11-18) and extended further throughout Chapter 4. As Jobes comments, "Personal knowledge of God and love for others as God defines it are inseparable. John's exhortation therefore implicitly demands self-examination."[13]

God sent his only Son into the world, so that through him we might have life – This sounds a lot like a summary of John 3:16:

---

16 "For God so loved the world that he gave his only and unique Son, so that everyone who trusts in him may have eternal life, instead of being utterly destroyed.

God sent his Son so that we might have life!

---

10. Jobes, *op. cit.,* 186.
11. Ibid., 190.
12. Johnson, *op. cit.,* 105.
13. Jobes, *op. cit.,* 190.

But he loved us and sent his Son to be the kapparah for our sins. - John is again using language and imagery from Yom Kippur, which we initially encountered in Chapter 2 (refer to the commentary on 2:2). Jobes adds, "Forgiveness of sin is at the heart of atonement and is the clearest expression of God's love."[14]

God is love - When we say "God is love," we need to be careful that we do not define love in a distorted or misunderstood way. For example, our society often has a distorted view of love. As David H. Stern points out, the phrase *God is love* "embodies the profoundest religious truth; yet it can be perverted into a callow slogan, in which God is pictured as some sort of floating fuzz-ball of love, accepting everything and judging nothing."[15]

Therefore, Jobes encourages, "Proper interpretation requires allowing John to define what he means by love."[16] For John, love is defined by "right behavior in relationships," as we will see in the following verses.

Furthermore, when we say "God is love," we must also take caution not to reverse that statement. The syntax of the Greek does not allow the statement to be inverted. Although we can say "God is love" we cannot say "love is God." There is a big difference![17] To again quote Jobes, "This tendency to define God by human concepts of love leads directly to self-serving heresy, such as is often presented in popular spirituality."[18]

---

14. Ibid., 193.
15. Stern, *op. cit.*, 775.
16. Jobes, *op. cit.*, 191.
17. For more on this, see Yarbrough, *op. cit.*, 237.
18. Jobes, *op. cit.*, 191.

vv. 11-16 – Loving One Another (Love in Action)

11 Beloved friends, if this is how God loved us, we likewise ought to love one another. **12** No one has ever seen God; if we love one another, God remains united with us, and our love for him has been brought to its goal in us. **13** Here is how we know that we remain united with him and he with us: he has given to us from his own Spirit. **14** Moreover, we have seen and we testify that the Father has sent his Son as Deliverer of the world. **15** If someone acknowledges that Yeshua is the Son of God, God remains united with him, and he with God. **16** Also we have come to know and trust the love that God has for us. God is love; and those who remain in this love remain united with God, and God remains united with them.

John continues his discussion on love for one another. The reason this is routinely emphasized by John, as Levertoff notes, is because, "The true test of love for Him is love for the brethren."[19]

He has given to us from his own Spirit – Keener comments:

Although the Qumran community as a group claimed to possess the Spirit, most of ancient Judaism relegated the Spirit's most dramatic works to the distant past and future, or to very rare individuals. For John, all true believers in Jesus have the Spirit, who moves them to love … and prophetically endows them to testify to the truth about Christ.[20]

19. Levertoff, *op. cit.,* 78.
20. Keener, *op. cit.,* 744.

vv. 17-18 – Love is an Antitode to Fear

17 Here is how love has been brought to maturity with us: as the Messiah is, so are we in the world. This gives us confidence for the Day of Judgment. **18** There is no fear in love. On the contrary, love that has achieved its goal gets rid of fear, because fear has to do with punishment; the person who keeps fearing has not been brought to maturity in regard to love.

Love has been brought to maturity – God's love has a transforming purpose in the lives of believers, and is a source of confidence and hope.

According to Jobes:

> The anaphoric article, "the love" (ἡ ἀγάπη), points backward and indicates that the love in view is that just previously mentioned in v. 16. Mutual love – God's for the believer and the believer's for God – comes to its fullest realization when a believer looks toward the day of judgement with confidence. This coheres with John's purpose to reassure his readers that they do in fact have eternal life because of their right belief in Jesus.[21]

There is no fear in love – John encourages his readers to not live in fear, especially in regard to the heavenly judgement. Why? Because "perfect love drives out fear." And the fear it specifically refers to is fear of punishment. Instead, as Jobes notes above, we can approach that day with confidence and the assurance of our salvation.

---

21. Jobes, *op. cit.*, 204.

Day of Judgment – This particular phrase does not appear in the Tanakh. Instead, we encounter the phrase "day of the Lord" (e.g., Isa. 13:6-13; Joel 1:15; 2:1; 3:4; 4:14; Amos 5:18-20; Obad. 15; Zeph. 1:17-18; Mal. 3:23). The phrase and concept of the "day of judgement" begins to appear in texts written during the Greco-Roman period (e.g., Judith 16:17; Jub. 5:10-14; T. Levi 3:2-3).[22]

vv. 19-21 – Love and Hate

19 We ourselves love now because he loved us first. **20** If anyone says, "I love God," and hates his brother [or sister], he is a liar. For if a person does not love his brother [or sister], whom they have seen, then they cannot love God, whom he has not seen. **21** Yes, this is the command we have from him: whoever loves God must love his brother too.

In these concluding verses of Chapter 4, John again challenges us regarding our love for one another, bringing the discussion full circle, which he introduced back in chapter 2 and picked up again in chapter 3 (2:9-11; 3:10 and 3:14-17).[23]

As Jobes rightly notes:

Ancient Israel's foremost command was the Shema, "Love the LORD your God with all you heart and with all your soul and with all your strength" (Deut. 6:5). Such love for God was coupled with obedience to the covenant, which included treating others rightly, both fellow Israelites and foreigners. John's argument is similar: love for God must be constituted by love for others, particularly fellow believers.[24]

22. Murray, *op. cit.,* 454.
23. Jobes, *op. cit.,* 206.
24. Ibid., 206.

If anyone says, "I love God," and hates his brother or sister, he is a liar – John contrasts love and hate, and by doing so, alludes back to the discussion about Cain in Chapter 3 where he associates hate with Cain (see the commentary to vv.11-18). Why Cain? Because, as previously mentioned, "In this context, everyone who hates their brother is like Cain, who hated his brother for living rightly before God."[25] John clearly states that a person who cannot love others cannot love God.

Reflection Questions

1. What does it mean to "test the spirits"?

2. Why is it important to be discerning about what we are taught? Why is this especially imperative for John and his audience?

3. What is "love in action"?

4. According to John, how does love serve to counter fear?

5. According to John, why is it impossible for a person to hate others but love God?

---

25. Ibid., 157.

1 JOHN
CHAPTER 5

Chapter five concludes John's first epistle. The opening verses return again to the common theme of love for God and one another. This emphasis is the primary hermeneutic for interpreting John's letters.

vv. 1-3 – Observance Flows from Our Love for God and One Another

---

1 Everyone who believes that Yeshua is the Messiah has God as his father, and everyone who loves a father loves his offspring too. **2** Here is how we know that we love God's children: when we love God, we also do what he commands. **3** For loving God means obeying his commands. Moreover, his commands are not burdensome,

---

Here is how we know that we love God's children: when we love God, we also do what he commands – According to John, we know we love his children (and therefore also God) when we rightly follow his commands. How is this so? Because embodied within the *mitzvot* of the Torah are detailed instructions for living a holy life – for being set apart unto God and being in healthy and proper relationships with one another. This is emphasized over and over throughout John's letters.

Paul Philip Levertoff writes:

> The essence of love is love for the divine essence in man. As the lightening breaks through the clouds, so does the hidden light of God break through the material veil of the world when there is love in us. As the sun scatters the darkness, so should our love lighten the dark and sad hearts. … As a father rejoices when his children are loved by others, so our heavenly father rejoices when we love even His prodigal sons and try to bring them back to the 'wings of the Shechinah."[1]

Karen H. Jobes further observes:

> On this reading, loving God and carrying out his commands is how we know that we love the children of God … it is another way of saying that we cannot define love for others until we obediently love God. In other words, "love is not defined instinctively but is rather revealed (3:16; 4:19), so that the knowledge that we love is grounded in the love of God and the keeping of his commandments."[2]

Moreover, his commands are not burdensome – Yeshua constantly emphasized a proper relationship to the Torah and the correct way to understand and apply the mitzvot in our daily lives. And when done appropriately and empowered by the Spirit, the commands are not a burden.

Matthew 11

28 "Come to me, all of you who are struggling and burdened, and I will give you rest. **29** Take my yoke upon you and learn from me, because I am gentle and humble in heart, and you will find rest for your souls. **30** For my yoke is easy, and my burden is light."

1. *Shechinah* is God's tangible presence. Levertoff, *op. cit.,* 46-47.
2. Jobes, *op. cit.,* 209.

Yeshua's use of the term "yoke" carries halachic nuance, referring to the weight of the commandments. This is confirmed by the way the same term (ζυγόν, *zygon*) is used in Acts 15:10 in reference to the decision to not require of Gentiles the same covenantal obligations as Jews to the mitzvot:

Acts 15:10, 19

10 So why are you putting God to the test now by placing a yoke on the neck of the disciples which neither our fathers nor we have had the strength to bear? ... 19 Therefore, my opinion is that we should not put obstacles in the way of the Gentiles who are turning to God.[3]

Furthermore, the encouragement that covenantal observance is not a burden is found within the Torah itself, for example:

Deuteronomy 30:11-14

11 For this command which I am giving you today is not too hard for you, it is not beyond your reach. 12 It isn't in the sky, so that you need to ask, 'Who will go up into the sky for us, bring it to us and make us hear it, so that we can obey it?' 13 Likewise, it isn't beyond the sea, so that you need to ask, 'Who will cross the sea for us, bring it to us and make us hear it, so that we can obey it?' 14 On the contrary, the word is very close to you - in your mouth, even in your heart; therefore, you can do it!

---

3. The "we" in this passage refers to the Jewish followers of Yeshua. Therefore, the decision made by the Jerusalem council was that although Gentiles are bound to certain matters of the Torah (i.e., *for Moses is taught in the synagogues every Shabbat - Acts 15:21*), ultimately, the same covenantal responsibility which remained incumbent upon Jews was not required of Gentiles. In regard to salvation there is no distinction, all are in need of redemption through Yeshua. However, there was a distinction in matters of the Torah's application and covenant-responsibility.

vv. 4-5 – Overcoming the World

4 because everything which has God as its Father overcomes the world. And this is what victoriously overcomes the world: our trust. **5** Who does overcome the world if not the person who believes that Yeshua is the Son of God?

We have spiritual victory and authority as children of God because of our faith in Yeshua.

And this is what victoriously overcomes the world: our trust – The word John uses for "trust" is πίστις *(pistis)*. Most other Bible translations render *pistis* as "faith." The corresponding Hebrew word is אמונה *(emunah)*. Both of these words can better be translated as "trusting-faithfulness." Through our faith/trust in God, through his Son, Yeshua, we have victory, the ability to overcome all of life's challenges, and ultimately receive our heavenly reward.

This is supported by Mark S. Kinzer, who although commenting specifically on the word "faith" as used in the Fourth Gospel, the meaning can consistently be applied to the letters, as well:

> John emphasizes "faith" as the proper response to the person and message of Yeshua. John writes his gospel with a clear and single purpose, and he conveys that purpose unambiguously at the end of the book: "But these [signs] are written so that you may come to believe that Yeshua is the Messiah, the Son of God, and that through believing you may have life in His name" (John 20:31).[4]

Yeshua is the Son of God – Jobes emphasizes, "John presses the identity of Jesus not simply as a great teacher, prophet, or even the

---

4. Kinzer, *Israel's Messiah and the People of God, op. cit.,* 146.

Messiah. He consistently identifies Jesus with God the Father, as God's Son who shares the divine nature (1:3, 7; 2:22-24; 3:8, 23; 4:9-10, 14, 15; 5:5, 9-13, 20)."[5]

vv. 6-8 – Water and Blood ... and Spirit

6 He is the one who came by means of water and blood, Yeshua the Messiah - not with water only, but with the water and the blood. And the Spirit bears witness, because the Spirit is the truth. 7 There are three witnesses - 8 the Spirit, the water and the blood - and these three are in agreement.

John is correcting a false teaching here, likely dealing with those who overemphasized the work of the Spirit while de-emphasizing the atoning role of Yeshua's sacrificial death.

Not with water only, but with the water and the blood – It appears John is refuting a claim by the secessionists that Yeshua came *"with water only."*

According to David H. Stern:

Contrary to gnostic teachings, he did not "receive the heavenly Christ" upon emerging from the Jordan; rather, it was Yeshua, already the Messiah, who was immersed; and his immersing in water symbolized his death and resurrection (see Ro 6:3-6). Likewise, he did not imitate being human but died a real death on the execution-stake; otherwise he would not have atoned for our sin. The blood, which is shorthand for Yeshua's death, witnesses that he is the Son of God (vv. 5, 9-13).[6]

---

5. Jobes, *op. cit.*, 217.
6. Stern, *op. cit.*, 776.

Water

John regularly uses water throughout his Gospel to symbolize both the Holy Spirit and purification/salvation. And in doing so, he is drawing directly from the Tanakh and the Jewish experience.

Isaiah 12:3

וּשְׁאַבְתֶּם-מַיִם בְּשָׂשׂוֹן מִמַּעַיְנֵי הַיְשׁוּעָה.

Then you will joyfully draw water from the wells of salvation.

Jobes confirms, "This symbolic use of water is a metaphor for the Spirit and also the constellation of associations that John makes with the Spirit, such as the impartation of truth and eternal life."[7]

Mark S. Kinzer breaks this imagery down even further:

John's linkage of purifying water and empowering Spirit echoes Ezekiel 36:24-28:

(24) I will take you from the nations, and gather you from all the countries, and bring you into your own land. (25) I will sprinkle clean water upon you, and you shall be clean from all your uncleannesses, and from all your idols I will cleanse you. (26) A new heart I will give you, and a new spirit I will put within you; and I will remove from your body the heart of stone and give you a heart of flesh. (27) I will put my Spirit within you, and make you follow my statutes and be careful to observe my ordinances. (28) Then you shall live in the land that I gave to your ancestors; and you shall be my people, and I will be your God.

---

7. Jobes, *op. cit.,* 219.

Ezekiel addresses Israel during the Babylonian exile, and proclaims what God will do for and among the people of Israel. God will bring Israel out of exile, and restore the people to its own land. This will vindicate the holiness of God's Name, by demonstrating God's power and covenant fidelity. But external restoration is insufficient, if unaccompanied by internal, relational, and behavioral transformation. So, God will sprinkle water of purification over his people (alluding to the Levitical rite of purification employing the ashes of the red heifer), to purify them from the defilement deriving from the sins that drove them into exile. Such ritual purification is essential, but it likewise is insufficient in itself. Consequently God will perfect the purification process by placing the divine Spirit within the people of Israel, which will empower them to live in covenant fidelity according to the statutes and ordinances of the Torah.[8]

Water therefore became an incredibly visual image linking Israel to God's redemption. That is why Yeshua then also makes the connection of water with salvation in John 4, in his encounter with the Samaritan woman at the well:

John 4:7-14

---

7 A woman from Shomron came to draw some water; and Yeshua said to her, "Give me a drink of water." **8** (His talmidim had gone into town to buy food.) **9** The woman from Shomron said to him, "How is it that you, a Jew, ask for water from me, a woman of Shomron?" (For Jews don't associate with people from Shomron.) **10** Yeshua answered her, "If you knew God's gift, that is, who it

---

8. Mar S. Kinzer, "Israel's Eschatological Renewal in Water and Spirit: A Messianic Jewish Perspective on Baptism." Paper prepared for the 2009 Messianic Jewish – Roman Catholic Dialogue Group (September 2009), 4.

is saying to you, 'Give me a drink of water,' then you would have asked him; and he would have given you living water." **11** She said to him, "Sir, you don't have a bucket, and the well is deep; so where do you get this 'living water'? **12** You aren't greater than our father Ya'akov, are you? He gave us this well and drank from it, and so did his sons and his cattle." **13** Yeshua answered, "Everyone who drinks this water will get thirsty again, **14** but whoever drinks the water I will give him will never be thirsty again! On the contrary, the water I give him will become a spring of water inside him, welling up into eternal life!"

This association with water, and its symbolism of life, salvation, and purification is most evident in, and at the heart of, the joyous Water Drawing Ceremony (*Simchat Beit HaShoeivah*) that took place during Sukkot[9] in the Second Temple period. Every day of the year, after the sacrifice was burned, an offering of wine was poured on the altar. But during Sukkot, there was also a water libation *(nisukh ha-mayim)*. Each day water was also poured on the special holiday offerings. Therefore, water had to be drawn by Levites and Priests from the Pool of Siloam and carried up to the Temple mount. This ceremony was accompanied by a joyous celebration as the water was paraded up to the Temple. The central verse at the heart of this ceremony was the one mentioned above, Isaiah 12:3: *"With joy shall you draw water from the wells of salvation."*

However, on the seventh day of Sukkot, on *Hoshanah Rabbah*,[10] the joys and festivities that accompanied the water drawing ceremony were exponentially increased, culminating

---

9. The Feast of Tabernacles. For a fuller description of this biblical holiday, please refer to the Glossary.
10. The Great Hosannah. For a fuller description, please refer to the Glossary.

with dancing, singing, and blasts of the shofar. Pious men danced with torches, scholars juggled, and the Levites played music while worshipers watched with excitement. The Temple courtyard was also specially furnished to accommodate the event, and even a balcony was set-up for women to be able to observe the celebrations.[11] It was such a monumental event that the Mishnah records: "The person who has not seen the joyous *Simchat Beit HaShoeivah* has never experienced true joy in his life."[12]

Drawing upon the imagery of this day Yeshua identified himself as the ultimate source of living water:

John 7:37-44

---

37 Now on the last day of the festival, *Hoshana Rabbah*, Yeshua stood and cried out, "If anyone is thirsty, let him come to me and drink! **38** Whoever puts his trust in me, as the Scripture says, rivers of living water will flow from his inmost being!"

Yeshua promises "living water" for all those who believe in him. In a desert environment it is easy to understand how water came to symbolize life, purification and salvation. Without water, it is impossible for life to exist. And in the same way, without the Spirit, it is impossible for vibrant spiritual life to exist.

Blood

Blood is of course a symbol both life and death, however it is more often used regarding death. John here uses "blood" as a reference to the physical nature of Yeshua, ultimately culminating in his sacrificial death.

---

11. *m. Sukkah* 5:2, 5; *b. Sukkah* 51a; and *b. Taanit* 2b-3a.
12. *m. Sukkah* 5:1 and *b. Sukkah* 51a.

He is the one who came by means of water and blood, Yeshua the Messiah - not with water only, but with the water and the blood - John is refuting the false teachers who were over-emphasizing the spiritual nature of Yeshua, saying he was revealed in *"water only."* John counters by emphasizing, *"not with water only, but with the water and the blood,"* referring to both Yeshua's deity and his physical incarnation, atoning death, and resurrection.

The one who came – According to Jobes, the use of the verb *come* (ἐλθών, *elthōn*) "suggests that the salvific mission of Jesus was achieved *both* by water and by blood, not water alone [italics hers]."[13]

Jobes then continues:

> John mentions water first because he *does* want to affirm the salvific connotation represented by "water" as a metaphor for the Spirit, but he also wants to add to it the essential element of "blood." The Spirit is essential because he applies atonement to the believer's life. But the blood is essential as the objective basis of that atonement. John *does* need to affirm the role of the Spirit in salvation, so he cannot say simply "not by water" and leave it at that. As a corrective statement it makes sense that John uses "water" in a double sense – first in reference to the way the false teaching about the Spirit is employing it, and then in a correction that refers to the water *and* the blood as symbols of the atoning life of Jesus [italics hers].[14]

Spirit

And the Spirit bears witness, because the Spirit is the truth ... the Spirit, the water and the blood - and these three are in

13. Jobes, *op. cit.*, 220.
14. Ibid., 220.

agreement – John solidifies his correction against the false teachers. As Jobes goes on to state: "John does not want to deny the role of the Spirit, but he anchors it in the historical life of Jesus, of whose significance the Spirit reminds [us] ... While the Spirit is necessary for salvation, his role is always coupled to and anchored in the earthly life of Jesus Christ, sent by the Father as an atoning sacrifice for sin."[15]

vv. 9-11 – True Witnesses

9 If we accept human witness, God's witness is stronger, because it is the witness which God has given about his Son. 10 Those who keep trusting in the Son of God have this witness in them. Those who do not keep trusting God have made him out to be a liar, because they have not trusted in the witness which God has given about his Son. 11 And this is the witness: God has given us eternal life, and this life is in his Son.

The above verses (vv.6-8) explain the three witnesses who testify on behalf of Yeshua: the Spirit, the Water, and the Blood. So why does John continue to refer to "witnesses" in this section? The reason is because John is thinking halachically. From a biblical and halachic perspective (and any legal or rational viewpoint) every claim must be supported either by evidence or witnesses.

Deuteronomy 19:15

"One witness alone will not be sufficient to convict a person of any offense or sin of any kind; the matter will be established only if there are two or three witnesses testifying against him.

---

15. Ibid., 221.

Matthew 18:16

> If he doesn't listen, take one or two others with you so that every accusation can be supported by the testimony of two or three witnesses.

2 Corinthians 13:1

> … Any charge must be established by the testimony of two or three witnesses.

In this discussion John asserts that his claims regarding Yeshua are valid and supported by witnesses: the Spirit, the Water, and the Blood. However, he also now appeals to an even stronger witness, God Himself.

And this is the witness: God has given us eternal life, and this life is in his Son – What these witnesses attest to is clear: "God has given us eternal life, and this life is in His Son (v.11)." This is why we can have the spiritual confidence described in the following verses.

vv. 12-15 – Confidence Through the Son

12 Those who have the Son have the life; those who do not have the Son of God do not have the life. **13** I have written you these things so that you may know that you have eternal life - you who keep trusting in the person and power of the Son of God. **14** This is the confidence we have in his presence: if we ask anything that accords with his will, he hears us. **15** And if we know that he hears us - whatever we ask - then we know that we have what we have asked from him.

Those who have the Son have the life – The exact meaning of "life" is discussed further in the commentary to 1:1, however, as Kinzer summarizes:

> In the apostolic tradition … "life" refers to a gift bestowed in the future, in the world to come (Matthew 7:14; 18:8-9; 19:16-17; 29; 25:46). Therefore, we might reasonably think that John's primary concern is to assure those who believe in Yeshua of their future destinies. However, close attention to John's usage makes clear that this is not the case. In John "eternal life" is received now, in *this* world. It is a present possession, not merely anticipated in the future … Eternal life is not merely Yeshua's gift to us – it is his presence among us and within us. This is why we need to "believe in" Yeshua in order to have that life – since "believing" means coming to him, loving him, remaining with him. When we draw near to Yeshua, we are drawing near to life. … This identification of Yeshua with "life" in John is linked to Yeshua's deity … To draw near to Yeshua is to draw near to God, and to draw near to God is to have life: "And this is eternal life, that they may know you, the only true God, and Yeshua the Messiah whom you have sent" (John 17:3).[16]

Those who do not have the Son of God do not have the life – In our post-modern world this is difficult to hear and understand. We are often uncomfortable with the idea that those who do not "have the Son of God" will not have eternal life. But Scripture is united on this, and why it is therefore incumbent upon us to share the life-giving power of our Messiah with those around us (c.f., Mark 16:15, Romans 1:16; *etc.*).

---

16. Kinzer, *Israel's Messiah and the People of God, op. cit.,* 147-148

vv. 16-18 – Confronting Sin

---

16 If anyone sees his brother committing a sin that does not lead to death, he will ask; and God will give him life for those whose sinning does not lead to death. There is sin that does lead to death; I am not saying he should pray about that. **17** All wrongdoing is sin, but there is sin that does not lead to death. **18** We know that everyone who has God as his Father does not go on sinning; on the contrary, the Son born of God protects him, and the Evil One does not touch him.

In these verses John discusses our responsibility to confront sin. However, these verses can also be a little confusing. What is "sin that <u>does not</u> lead to death"? And what does he mean by "sin that <u>does</u> lead to death"?

If anyone sees his brother committing a sin – We have a personal responsibility to confront blatant sin in other believers in Yeshua. How do we do that? The appropriate way to do so is the process laid out in Matthew 18:15-17. However, when we do so, we need to first make sure our own spiritual lives are in order, and that the truth we speak is not being done out of self-righteousness or judgement. Instead, our correction should be based out of love. Sadly, this is difficult, because often sin is confronted in hurtful and harming ways. Sin must be addressed, otherwise it affects not only the individual(s) but the community as a whole. However, when we do address sin, let's make sure our intentions are restorative and in pursuit of ultimate spiritual health.

Stern adds, "A believer's responsibility to *a brother committing sin* is not only to ask God to *give him life*, but also to 'go and show him his fault' (Mt 18:15-17), to 'set him right, but in a spirit of humility' (Ga 6:1), to 'turn' him 'from his wandering path' (Jam 5:19-20)."[17]

Sin that does <u>not</u> lead to death – As noted below, in the context of 1 John "death" is spiritual separation from God. Therefore, John is saying that there are two kinds of sin – those that hinder our relationship with God, and those which completely sever our relationship with God.

As discussed in the commentary to 1 John 1:8-10 the Hebrew word *Chet* (חֵטְא), which is usually translated as "sin," better means to "miss the mark." It is to veer off-course from the path of proper spiritual, moral and ethical behavior.[18] The answer to these kinds of sins is *Teshuva* (תְּשׁוּבָה), to return/repent.

However, there are other sins that have far greater consequences, as we'll see below.

Sin that <u>does</u> lead to death – This refers to sin that prevents a person from attaining eternal life. According to Jobes:

> In the context of 1 John the sin that leads to death must be related to the statement in 5:12, "The one who has the Son has life; the one who does not have the Son of God does not have life" and therefore on the path that leads to death. ... Sin that leads to death is that which excludes one from the realm of life, sin that prevents one from having the Son.[19]

It's important to point out here, as we look at the whole chapter and letter, John's purpose is to reassure his readers of their eternal life, not discourage them into doubting their salvation.

The Torah itself notes that there are different kinds of sin, evident in the different types of resolutions. Some sins simply

---

17. Stern, *op. cit.,* 777.
18. Wayne Dosick, *Living Judaism* (New York: Harper Collins, 1995), 139.
19. Jobes, *op. cit.,* 235-236.

require confession and a possible offering and/or sacrifice. Others have more severe punishments associated with them. The harshest form of punishment in the Torah (aside from death/stoning) is כרת (karet), exile from the community, because being exiled (or more literally, "cut off") from the community also means being exiled/cut-off from the presence of God. This is the "death" referred to by John – separation from the realm of eternal life (Numbers 15:30-31).

Within the Tanakh, examples of sins resulting in karet include those who intentionally eat chametz on Passover (Ex. 12:15, 19), who engage in certain sexual violations (Lev. 18:29), and those who distain male circumcision (Gen. 17:14). Later in time, the Mishnah (Keritot 1.1) identified thirty-six different offences incurring karet.

Stern notes:

> Judaism distinguishes between unconscious sin, for which sacrifices atone, and deliberate, "high-handed" sin, for which only death atones. In the context of this letter, those who deliberately choose not to "keep trusting in the person and power of the Son of God" (v.13), who do not obey God's commands (vv.2-3) and who do not love their brothers (4:21), "do not have life" (v.12).[20]

Craig S. Keener further comments:

> The Old Testament and Judaism distinguished between willful rebellion against God, which could not be forgiven by normal means, and a lighter transgression. More relevant here, some ancient Jewish texts (e.g., the Dead Sea Scrolls, Jubilees) also spoke of a capital offense as "a matter of death," which was normally enforced by excommunication from the community rather than literal execution.[21]

---

20. Stern, op. cit., 777.
21. Keener, op. cit., 745.

Everyone who has God as his Father does not go on sinning –
John again states for a second time (echoing 3:9) that a person
who has been born of God does not sin. According to Jobes, the
parallel phrases in 3:9 and 5:8 "suggest that the same sin or type
of sin is in view. As argued above, that sin is lawlessness (ἀνομία),
a rejection of God's authority to define sin and, consequently, a
rejection of God's grace."[22]

And the Evil One does not touch him – Keener points out, "Satan
could not touch Job without God's permission (Job 1:11-12; 2:2-
6). Judaism recognized that Satan needed God's permission to test
God's people, and that God rejected Satan's accusations against
God's own people."[23]

vv. 19-20 – Understanding Spiritual Identity

19 We know that we are from God, and that the whole world lies
in the power of the Evil One. **20** And we know that the Son of God
has come and has given us discernment, so that we may know who
is genuine; moreover, we are united with the One who is genuine,
united with his Son Yeshua the Messiah. He is the genuine God
and eternal life.

John starts to close his letter by referencing the duality of God
and "the Evil One," but encourages us that through discernment
given to as followers of Yeshua, we are able to overcome these
influences (including those of the false-teachers) that separate us
from God.

---

22. Jobes, *op. cit.,* 237.
23. Keener, *op. cit.,* 745.

So that we may know who is genuine – According to Jobes:

To know "the True One" is to be "in" him through his Son, Jesus Christ. This concept is similar to the apostle Paul's idea of union in Christ (Rom 6:5; 1 Cor 6:17; Phil 2:1). To be "in Christ" is to be joined to his eternal life, his destiny; this is the basis for Jesus' statement, "Because I live, you also will live" (John 14:19).[24]

v. 21 – Final Warning Against False Teachers

---

21 Children, guard yourselves against false gods!

This abrupt concluding statement is a reminder of the purpose of John's letter, which was not only to be a source of encouragement, but to also confront false teaching and those who broke away from the community. As Jobes notes, "In the historical situation of that moment, John was likely alluding to the false ideas about God that were being taught by the secessionists."[25]

That interpretation is supported by Colin G. Kruse, as well:

What does seem clear is that in the immediate context keeping oneself from idols is the necessary concomitant of knowing the true God through Jesus Christ. But in the context of the letter as a whole it is not the pagans who do not know the true God, but the secessionists (cf. 1:6; 2:4). For this reason … it is an exhortation not to accept the false teaching of the secessionists.[26]

---

24. Jobes, *op. cit.,* 241.
25. Ibid., 243.
26. Kruse, *op. cit.,* 202.

The sudden ending to John's letter has led some modern readers to speculate whether an original ending was lost. However, Jobes counters:

> [T]here is no manuscript evidence to support such a conjecture. But the original recipients would most likely have seen this "punchline" as a rhetorically powerful ending that demanded a response to the implied question, "Whom will you serve? The one true God or idols, who represent only false idea, darkness, and death?"[27]

Conclusion

John wrote his letters to confront a split over conflicting theologies and behavioral concerns. Certain individuals broke away from the network of congregations under John's care and authority and were traveling around attempting to influence others with their false teachings. John's primary concern was to both encourage and warn all those who looked to him for guidance.

Although John wrote to address these particular pastoral concerns, he also wrote to provide hope, encouragement, and guidance. His letters also provide significant contributions on a number of key theological issues and themes which remain relevant to the present day.

First and foremost is John's hermeneutic for interpreting everything in Scripture, our love for God and our love for one another. This understanding must always influence the way we read and interpret his writings.

John also wrote not only to address those who broke away and their false teachings, but to also instruct his audience about the

---

27. Jobes, *op. cit.,* 242.

correct way to understand who Yeshua is, but also how we are to conduct our lives, and our assurance of eternal life.

According to John, our observance should flow out of love, for God and one another. We should be confident in our spiritual journey (our salvation) through our faith in Yeshua and the work of the Spirit. Furthermore, God gives us the ability to overcome … not for perfection … but ultimate spiritual victory.

Reflection Questions

1. How do we ensure that our observance flows out of love?

2. How can we be assured of eternal life?

3. What are ways (both positive and negative) you've experienced confrontation of sin? What you can you learn from that/those experience(s)?

4. How are we supposed to understand our spiritual identity in Messiah?

5. After studying through 1 John, what has changed in your perspective of the letter? Is there anything new you have learned?

2 JOHN

John's second letter is only thirteen verses long. Unlike 1 John, which is more of a treatise or written sermon, 2 and 3 John are true letters, written in the characteristic style of ancient correspondence. It begins with a description of who it's from, to whom it is addressed, and has a personal conclusion.

The letter basically encapsulates the situation and problems of 1 John. However, in doing so, it also does not seem to add anything we don't already know from the previous letter. Which then begs the question: why was it written?

The purpose of John's second letter is two-part: To encourage the recipients in their faith and observance, especially in how they treat one another (vv.5-6); and to address the problem of itinerant teachers whose instruction he considered dangerous and false (v.10).

According to Marianne Meye Thompson:

> It is possible that 2 John served as a cover letter, sent along with 1 John, to include personal greetings from the Elder to a specific congregation in his care. It is also possible that 1 and 2 John were intended for different audiences: 1 John was circulated in the Elder's immediate vicinity, while 2 John was

sent to those at a distance, whom the Elder could contact only by letter (v.12) or by messenger (v.4). In any case, it is safe to say that the two letters illumine each other and are so obviously written with the same situation in view that each may be used to interpret the other.[1]

Craig S. Keener adds:

Second John may function as an official letter, the sort that high priests could send to Jewish leaders outside Palestine. The length is the same as that of 3 John; both were probably limited to this length by the single sheet of papyrus on which they were written; in contrast to most New Testament letters, most other ancient letters were of this length.[2]

Outline of 2 John

1-2	Address of the Letter
3	Formal Greetings
4-6	Love and Observance
7-11	Warning against False Teachers
12-13	Closing

vv. 1-2 – Address of the Letter

1 From: The Elder. To: The chosen lady and her children, whom I love in truth - and not only I but also all who have come to know the truth - **2** because of the truth which remains united with us and will be with us forever:

1. Thompson, *op. cit.,* 150.
2. Keener, *op. cit.,* 747.

The Elder - πρεσβύτερος in Greek, or 'presbyter' is a term that literally means "old man," similar to the Hebrew word זקן *zaken*. However, it can refer to either an older (and therefore venerable) person, or a specific leader, regardless of age.[3] As Karen H. Jobes confirms:

> [T]he adjectival form 'elder' used as a substantive (πρεσβύτερος [*presbyteros*]), found here, is used dozens of times in the NT to refer to the religious leaders of Jewish congregations (e.g., Matt. 21:23; Mark 8:31; Luke 22:52), and it has continued to be used to designate leaders in the [believing community] (e.g., Acts 14:23; 1 Peter 5:1).

> This distinction in usage between the noun and adjective likely indicates that, regardless of the elder's age, the designation implies the author's authority in the church(es) to which he writes (c.f. 1 John 1:1). ... The author's identification simply as 'the elder' implies both the position of authority he held and the personal relationship he had with the original recipients.[4]

The chosen lady and her children (Ἐκλεκτῇ κυρίᾳ, *eklektē kyria*) - The congregation to which John is writing is designated metaphorically as *the chosen lady and her children*. Thompson points out that the New Testament elsewhere speaks of the faith community as a woman or bride, and when greetings are sent from *the children of the chosen sister* (v.13), it suggests greetings sent from one congregation to another.[5] Such personification is drawn directly from the Tanakh and Apocrypha where Israel is often referred to as a wife, bride, mother and daughter.[6] David H.

---

3. Julie Galambush. "The Second Letter of John," *The Jewish Annotated New Testament*, Ed. Amy-Jill Levine and Marc Zvi Brettler (New York: Oxford, 2011), 456.
4. Jobes, *op. cit.*, 255.
5. Thompson, *op. cit.*, 151.
6. Kruse, *op. cit.*, 204.

Stern adds that this may have been a way to disguise who the letter was addressed to avoid scrutiny and Roman censorship.[7]

Some have tried to interpret this address literally, meaning that John intended for this letter to be delivered to a specific woman and her actual physical children. However, such a literal reading is rejected by most scholars for various grammatical reasons, common usage at the time, and coherence of the text itself.[8]

The word *truth* (ἀλήθεια, *alétheia*) is mentioned four times in the first three verses alone, and is repeated throughout the letter. Jobes notes, "Living in the truth is the common theme among all three letters; it comes to its sharpest expression in the elder's concern for the health and unity of the [community] – especially when some are *not* living in the truth [italics hers]."[9]

Strong's defines *alétheia* as "truth, but not merely truth as spoken; [but] truth of idea, reality, sincerity, truth in the moral sphere, divine truth revealed to [humanity], straightforwardness."[10] John's use of the word in these first two verses specifically implies the reality of Yeshua and the Gospel message.

N.T. Wright explains:

> Truth, for John, seems to be something to do with a wholeness, a completeness, of human life, from the stirrings of thought and imagination through to every detail of practical living. He believes that in Jesus the Messiah the creator God has both displayed the form and pattern of this truth and, by dealing with all the untruth in the world, all the lies that distort and deface humans and the world, has enabled men and women to

---

7. Stern, *op. cit.,* 778.
8. For further explanations to support this, see: Yarbrough, *op. cit.,* 333-334, Jobes, *op. cit.,* 255-256; Kruse, *op. cit.,* 204-205; among others.
9. Jobes, *op. cit.,* 247.
10. *Strong's Concordance of the Bible.* Accessed via biblehub.com (March 30, 2019) - https://biblehub.com/greek/225.htm

rediscover truth-in-action, truth-in-the-heart, truth-in-real-life. Truth has to do with integrity. And integrity has to do with God's redeeming purposes for the whole world, with God's plan for the new creation.

Truth, then, isn't just a matter of saying things which correspond to reality, saying 'today it is cold' when it really is. That is simply surface-level truth. Truth, for John, is something that goes down deep and spreads out wide. It is what happens when humans, redeemed in the Messiah and renewed by the Spirit, think, speak, and act in a way which corresponds to God's plan to renew the whole creation – and, indeed, which sets that renewal forward in whatever way they are called to do.[11]

v. 3 – Formal Greeting

3 Grace, mercy and shalom will be with us from God the Father and from Yeshua the Messiah, the Son of the Father, in truth and love.

Steven J. Kraftchick notes, "Ancient Jewish letter writers used the phrase 'mercy and peace' to express their desire that the divine blessing of *hesed* and *shalom* rest on the letter's recipients always and forever."[12] John's formulation bears a close resemblance to this common Jewish blessing, but adds the Greek word χάρις (*charis*, grace), perhaps to further include and distinguish between the Hebrew words רחמים (*rachamim*, compassion) and חסד (*chesed*, mercy), which are both often translated as 'mercy.' John may have

---

11. Wright, *The Early Christian Letters for Everyone, op. cit.,* 175.
12. Kraftchick, *op. cit.,* 28.

wanted to emphasize grace, and its being from, and connected to the truth of Yeshua.

From God the Father and from Yeshua the Messiah, the Son of the Father – John's greeting includes an emphasis on the special relationship (and differentiation) between Yeshua and "the Father." By emphasizing this, John is clearly indicating that Yeshua is more than just an earthly or human Messiah. Hershel Shanks explains:

> "By Jesus' time ... the concept of the *mashiach* had developed beyond that of an earthly messiah who would restore the glory of the kingdom of David. It also came to mean a divinely sent figure who would return as God's agent and usher in the world to come. The Dead Sea Scrolls reflect this development... thus...the messiah was already freighted with eschatological content."[13]

Shanks further adds, "that divine sonship is present in the Dead Sea Scrolls before Jesus is declared the Son of God should not be surprising."[14] John intentionally associates the concepts of *"Messiah"* and *"Son of the Father"* together in Yeshua to accentuate his divine status. And this should not be understood as a break with wider Jewish messianic expectation.

The earliest Jewish followers did not see themselves as practicing idolatry, or worshiping a foreign god by proclaiming Yeshua's divinity. According Larry Hurtado, "all evidence indicates, however, that those Jewish [believers] who made such a step remained convinced that they were truly serving the God of the Old Testament."[15] He further elucidates:

---

13. Hershel Shanks, *The Mystery and Meaning of the Dead Sea Scrolls* (New York: Random House, 1998), 68-69.

14. Ibid., 69.

15. Larry W. Hurtado, *One God, One Lord: Early Christian Devotion and Ancient Jewish Monotheism* (Philadelphia: Fortress Press, 1998), 14.

The cultic veneration of Jesus as a divine figure apparently began among Jewish [believers], whose religious background placed great emphasis upon the uniqueness of God. It is evident that their devotion had its own distinct shape, a kind of binitarian reverence which included both God and the exalted Jesus ... apparently they regarded this redefinition not only as legitimate, but, indeed, as something demanded of them.[16]

John concludes his greeting with another emphasis on "truth" and "love," themes regularly repeated throughout his writings and which we will further unpack below.

vv. 4-6 – Love and Observance

4 I was very happy when I found some of your children living in truth, just as the Father commanded us. 5 And now, dear lady, I am requesting that we love one another - not as if this were a new command I am writing you, for it is the one which we have had from the beginning. 6 Moreover, love is this: that we should live according to his commands. This is the command, as you people have heard from the beginning; live by it!

Living in truth - John now shares his joy in receiving reports that this community (or group of communities) is living faithfully. John specifically uses the phrase *"living in the truth,"* which as Jobes notes, is a "distinctly Johannine metaphor; it means to live in a way consistent with the revelation Jesus Christ has brought (cf. 1 John 1:6; 3 John 3-4).[17] Or as Kruse describes, "To walk in

16. Ibid., 11.
17. Jobes, *op. cit.,* 261.

the truth means to live in accordance with the truth of the message of the gospel as it was received in the beginning."[18]

Which we have had from the beginning. - The commandment John mentions here is an "old law" (i.e. *"from the beginning"*) because it from the Torah *(love your neighbor as yourself* - Lev. 19:18), however Yeshua's regular emphasis gave it unique importance (see especially Matthew 22:36-40 and John 13:34-35).

In the context of 1 and 2 John, "loving one another" includes hospitality extended to others, especially traveling emissaries, and cleaving to the community (rather than leaving it, as the secessionists were doing).[19]

But John's instructions here are more than just an encouragement to treat one another respectfully. John intentionally connects love with observance. As Stern notes, "For loving one another includes all the commands."[20] This is also the position of the great 19th century Jewish believer, Rabbi Yechiel Tzvi Lichtenstein, who in his monumental commentary in Hebrew[21] on the New Testament, comments:

לאהבה איש את רעהו ... כי זה כולל כל המיצוות.

Love one another ... for this encompasses all of the mitzvot.[22]

According to John, love and observance must always go together. They are two side of the same coin. This is why John regularly records variations of Yeshua's words: *"If you love me, you will*

18. Kruse, *op. cit.,* 207.
19. Keener, *op. cit.,* 749.
20. Stern, *op. cit.,* 778.
21. Originally published in consecutive volumes between 1891-1904 in Leipzig, Germany.
22. Yechiel Tzvi Lichtenstein, *Sugiyot Nivcharot B'sefer HaBrit HaChadashah* (Jerusalem: Keren Ahavah Meshichit, 2002), 359 [translation mine].

keep my commands (John 14:15-24). " The "commands" are, of course, the commandments of the Torah given to the Jewish people. Julie Galambush confirms, "In the Tanakh there is no opposition between loving God and observing the commandments, and both are equated with walking in God's ways (see Deut. 30:16)."[23]

This connection of love with observance is found directly in the Torah itself. Therefore, to understand the Bible's use of the word love, we need to understand the context in which it is regularly used. In the Bible, love is covenantal language. It is more than a feeling, it is a commitment. It is a verb, an action. For example, the *Shema* (Deuteronomy 6) states:

ד שְׁמַע יִשְׂרָאֵל: יי אֱלֹהֵינוּ יי אֶחָד.	**4** Hear, O Israel: the LORD our God, the LORD is one.
ה וְאָהַבְתָּ אֵת יי אֱלֹהֶיךָ בְּכָל-לְבָבְךָ וּבְכָל-נַפְשְׁךָ וּבְכָל-מְאֹדֶךָ.	**5** And you shall love the LORD your God with all your heart, with all your soul, and with all your might.

Mark S. Kinzer explains:

> Deuteronomy 6:4-9 plays a prominent role in the life and teaching of Yeshua. He views it as the first and greatest commandment, and links it to the commandment in the Torah to love one's neighbor (Leviticus 19:18). This linkage does not add to the Shema but interprets it: all attempts at loving God that compromise love of neighbor are proven fraudulent.

> In John Yeshua applies God's command to love one's neighbor to the mutual love required of his disciples, and presents "laying down one's life" as the ultimate expression of such love. This is what Yeshua himself does for his own in

---

23. Galambush, *op. cit.,* 457.

129

willing fulfillment of his Father's commandment, and thus the disciples' love for one another participates in their Master's sacrificial self-giving. Yeshua's obedience to his Father in laying down his life bears witness to his wholehearted love of God:

The ruler of this world is coming. He has no claim on me; rather, this is happening so that the world may know that I love the Father and that I do as the Father has commanded me. (John 14:30-31)

Yeshua's suffering and death thus embodies perfectly the love of God and neighbor required by the Shema.[24]

Therefore, when the Torah tells us that we are to *love God with all of our heart, with all of our soul, and with all of our might*, it means we are to follow God, adhere to His mitzvot, and live in covenantal obedience. Loving God is not about having "warm, fuzzy feelings" (although that's nice), but rather obedience and self-sacrifice. It is a commitment to follow God even when we don't feel like it or when we have doubts.

vv. 7-11 – Warning Against False Teachers

7 For many deceivers have gone out into the world, people who do not acknowledge Yeshua the Messiah's coming as a human being. Such a person is a deceiver and an anti-Messiah. **8** Watch yourselves, so that you won't lose what you have worked for, but will receive your full reward. **9** Everyone who goes ahead and does not remain true to what the Messiah has taught does not have God. Those who remain true to his teaching have both the Father and the Son. **10** If someone comes to you and does not bring this

---

24. Kinzer, *Israel's Messiah and the People of God, op. cit.,* 70.

teaching, don't welcome him into your home. Don't even say, "Shalom!" to him; **11** for the person who says, "Shalom!" to him shares in his evil deeds.

Here is John's secondary (and some argue, primary) purpose in writing his letter: to address the same issue which he further expanded upon in the first letter, specifically, to deal with the problem of itinerant teachers whose teaching the Elder (v.1) judges to be false (v.10) because it denies that *Messiah Yeshua has come in the flesh* (v.7 and 1 John 4:2).[25]

The exhortation to love one another by walking in the truth is juxtaposed with the many deceivers who are not walking in the truth. As Jobes explains:

> This ties the elder's concern back to the same concern in 1 John (2:18-23; 3:7; 4:3). In all the books of the NT, only John's letters mention the word "antichrist," and that shared word ties 1 John and 2 John together historically. The initial conjunction "for" (Ὅτι causal) shows that the discussion of Christology is integrally related to the exhortation to love in v.6."[26]

The author uses the term "anti-Messiah" in verse 7 as a neologism (see also 1 John 2:18 and 4:3) to indicate that the opponents are literally "against the Messiah," rather than a reference to a specific satanic agent.[27]

John warns his readers against participating in their *evil deeds* (v.11) by accepting their beliefs or aiding their propaganda in any way.[28] For these teachers, he writes, have *gone out into the world*

---

25. Thompson, *op. cit.,* 149.
26. Jobes, *op. cit.,* 264.
27. Galumbush, *op. cit.,* 457.
28. Thompson, 149.

(v.7 and 1 Jn 2:18-19), indicating that they are former community members who have left and are now probably trying to win over others to their teaching.[29]

The specific teaching addressed is the same as in 1 John - the deceivers "*do not acknowledge Yeshua the Messiah's coming as a human being* (v.7)" and have left the circle of communities under John's care and authority (1 John 2:19), and are attempting to influence others. The issue is the belief that Yeshua did not come in the flesh.

Jobes points out, "The present participle 'coming' (ἐρχόμενον) refers not to a future coming, such as the second coming of Christ, but to the past event of the incarnation."[30] She goes on to emphasize:

> True knowledge of God is found only in the incarnation of Jesus Christ, for the Word became flesh specifically to reveal the otherwise invisible God (John 1:18). Therefore, everyone who has a true knowledge of God acknowledges that 'Jesus Christ has come in the flesh'; that is, the Son of God became a human being. Certainly this truth would argue against Docetism, but also more broadly against many forms of christological error.

> The particular phrase "has come in the flesh" suggests that the debate of concern to the elder probably involved the means of salvation more than the nature of Jesus Christ ... the verb 'to come' in Johannine Christological contexts not only means (denotes) 'to appear on the scene' but also signifies (connotes) 'to act salvifically' (see John 5:43; 7:28; 8:42; 12:46; 16:28; 18:37). While sound Christology certainly insists on the

---

29. Ibid., 149-150.
30. Jobes, *op. cit.,* 264.

physical incarnation of Christ as fully human, Christ's full humanity was necessary *because of* his role in God's plan of salvation as the atoning sacrifice for sin [italics hers].[31]

Therefore, verse 11 warns against even greeting a person who teaches contrary to this because greetings were an essential part of the social protocol at the time, and the greeting (*Shalom aleichem*, *'Peace be upon you'*) was intended as a blessing or prayer to impart peace.[32]

According to Keener:

> In the Dead Sea Scrolls, one who provided for an apostate from the community was regarded as an apostate sympathizer and was expelled from the community, as the apostate was. Housing or blessing a false teacher was thus seen as collaborating with him.[33]

This is similarly supported in a quote from *Avot de Rabbi Natan*:

> He who joins himself to those who commit transgressions, though he does not do what they do, will nevertheless receive punishment as one of them (30).[34]

vv. 12-13 – Closing

---

12 Although I have much to write you people, I would rather not use paper and ink. Instead, I hope to come and see you and to talk with you face to face, so that our joy may be complete. **13** The children of your chosen sister send you their greetings.

---

31. Ibid., 264-265.
32. Keener, *op. cit.,* 749.
33. Ibid., 749.
34. An 8th-10th century aggadic work, as cited in: Galumbush, *op. cit.,* 457.

"Paper" is of course papyrus, made from reeds and rolled up like a scroll. The pen was a reed pointed at the end, and the ink was a compound of charcoal, vegetable gum and water.[35] Keener explains, "Written letters were considered an inferior substitution for personal presence or for a speech, and writers sometimes concluded their letters with the promise to discuss matters further face-to-face."[36]

The children of your chosen sister – This, of course, is a reference to the members of John's community where he is writing from and based, likely the Ephesus congregation and its close affiliates. For more on John's use of "chosen sister/lady" as references to communities rather than specific individuals, see the commentary on vv.1-2 above.

Conclusion

John's wrote his second letter to encourage these believers in their faith and observance, especially in how they treat one another (vv.5-6); and to address the problem of itinerant teachers whose instruction he considered dangerous and false (v.10).

According to John, our observance of the *mitzvot* should flow out of love ... our love for God and for one another. As the great sage Hillel taught, "All the rest is commentary."[37] Therefore, if our pursuit of Torah and its observance is not drawing us closer to God and into deeper, healthier relationships, then something is wrong. Clearly it is not the Torah's instructions, but rather our approach and understanding of them.

---

35. Keener, *op. cit.,* 749.
36. Ibid., 749.
37. *b. Shabbat 31a*

We all know individuals (from all types of religious backgrounds) who just "go through the motions." They may even be the most observant people we know, but their lives and relationships are a wreck. Although none of us are perfect, the Torah (and all of Scripture) should be shaping us into a greater reflection of our Messiah. If Yeshua is the Living Torah, the perfect embodiment of God's instructions in the Torah (the "Word made flesh"), then our observance should emulate his. Our observance should cause us to generally be more patient and kind, concerned with those who are less fortunate and on the fringes, and bold in our faith, declaring to the world Yeshua's messiahship. Proper observance of the *mitzvot* must result in a deeper, healthier, and growing faith. If our lives are not producing fruit than we need to completely reassess how we understand and apply God's instructions. This is why it is extremely important to be a part of a healthy community and guided by a recognized and informed rabbi or leader.

This is also why it is very important to avoid being led astray. Not only in our observance but also in our theologies. We need to stay true to the foundations of our faith and a proper understanding of who Yeshua is and what he has done for us. Because errors in the fundamentals can have serious spiritual ramifications.

John warns us to use discernment regarding false-teachers and the abuse of spiritual authority. He also implores us to remain faithful in a difficult world. To not give into temptations around us, but to remain focused on "living in truth." And for those who are faithful in doing so, eternal rewards await them from our Father in heaven.

Furthermore, the Second Epistle of John should also remind us to live *now* for the return of Messiah. Our theologies should shape our interactions with the world, one another, and with God. Every day we should be expecting the return of Messiah ... in thought and in deed.

This is also why John emphasizes the importance of community. Our lives are intimately linked together with those around us, and false teaching and improper behavior are dangerous because they affect all of us. That is why we must remain focused and committed to one another and producing spiritual fruit.[38]

Reflection Questions

1. Why did John write this letter?

2. What is the connection between love and observance?

3. Why do you think John was so concerned about false teaching?

4. If we are supposed to be careful regarding false teachers and errant teachings, how do we know whether something is false or in error? Are there specific details we should be watching for? What else can help us in proper living and theology?

5. If you were one of the members of the congregation that received this letter, would you have taken John's counsel seriously?

6. Is this book still relevant today, and if so, why and how?

---

38. Galatians 5:22-23

3 John

Third John is the shortest book in the New Testament, less than 200 words in the original Greek text, and just 14 verses in English. It would have fit on a single papyrus sheet.[1]

The progression of John's Letters, as N.T. Wright notes, provides a "zooming-in effect."[2] The first letter was more universal and widely applicable. It could have been addressed to almost any congregation. Whereas the second letter was written to a specific congregation and more directly addressed issues alluded to in the first letter, but applied in the context of a specific community. John's third letter was even more focused, written to a particular leader within a specific congregation dealing with very direct issues and people.

Third John is a private letter written to an individual named Gaius.[3] As such, it stands apart from other New Testament epistles in being "closer in form and structure to other extant personal notes from the ancient world."[4] Karen H. Jobes explains:

---

1. Jobes, *op. cit.,* 281
2. Wright, *The Early Christian Letters for Everyone, op. cit.,* 183-184.
3. Kruse, *op. cit.,* 219
4. Jobes, *op. cit.,* 282.

Just as there are various types of letters in the modern world that take different forms depending on their purpose and the relationship between the writer and recipient – compare a business form to letter to a chatty email from a close friend – different kinds of personal correspondence from the ancient world are known among the extant documentary papyri.[5]

It is basically a "letter of recommendation" and a reference for Demetrius, a traveling emissary (vv.7-8) who needs to be put up and supported by a local community while serving in the area.[6] It is also an encouragement to Gaius to continue extending hospitality to traveling emissaries, especially those who come from the apostle John or who are loyal to him.[7]

John's third letter additionally serves as a rebuke of another leader, Diotrephes, who is apparently exerting considerable influence, and has placed himself in opposition to John and failing to support and extend hospitality to his emissaries. John already sent at least one letter to Diotrephes (v.9), which was apparently ignored, so he is now reaching out to Gaius to undertake the hospitality that Diotrephes has refused to do (vv.9-10).[8]

We should also note that 3 John is the only New Testament book that does not directly mention Yeshua by name (see more on this in the commentary to verse 7). However, as Jobes highlights, given its brevity and specific purpose, this should not be too surprising.[9]

It should also not be lost on us that we are reading an actual note from the apostle John, and that Demetrius would have carried

---

5. Ibid, 282.
6. Keener, *op. cit.,* 750.
7. Thompson, *op. cit.,* 158.
8. Ibid., 158.
9. Jobes, *op. cit.,* 281.

this with him to give to Gaius.[10] Although it may seem easy to assume that 3 John is insignificant, and not worth our attention, I want to challenge that assumption. 3 John provides a peak into John's life and what his private correspondence was like. Not just the stuff he wrote for a broader audience, but also what he wrote to individual acquaintances. It shares a little of who he was as a person and his relationships. This very short letter also helps us understand the kinds of tensions he faced, and the rifts that were already happening between early communities and leaders.

Imagine when you read this letter that you are back in the first century … and you have just learned that the authority of an actual disciple of Yeshua is being dismissed. This should come as quite a shock!

Outline of 3 John

1	Address of the Letter
2-4	Formal Greeting
5-8	Gaius Commended for His Hospitality
9-10	Rebuke of Diotrephes
11	Further Encouragement to Gaius
12	Recommendation of Demetrius
13-14	Closing

v. 1 – Address of the Letter

---

1 From: The Elder. To: Dear Gaius, whom I love in truth:

---

10. Yarbrough, *op. cit.,* 363.

Like 2 John, 3 John is a true letter, written in the characteristic formal style of ancient correspondence. It immediately tells us who it's from, to whom it is addressed, and has a personal conclusion. According to Jobes:

> The address of the letter was always the first line of a letter, identifying both the writer and the recipient. The writer of 3 John identifies himself only as "the elder" and writes to a dear acquaintance whose name is Gaius. Knowing that this book originated as personal correspondence provides a key to interpreting its message because we can be assured that the issues it addresses and the names it mentions refer to authentic people and the given situation was real.

The Elder - πρεσβύτερος in Greek, or 'presbyter.' It literally means "old man" but is used more specifically to refer to an office (similar to the Hebrew word זקן *zaken*). For more on this, see the commentary to 2 John 1-2.

"Dear Gaius, whom I love in truth" – The Latin name Gaius (which means "rejoicing") was a common name in the Greco-Roman world.

Wright explains:

> [John] is writing to one particular [congregational] leader, someone called Gaius about whom, sadly, we don't know anything else. We don't know which [congregation] he belonged to, or why he received this short letter. But we do know enough to be able to learn a couple of much-needed lessons from what John has to say to him.[11]

What little information we have about Gaius has not stopped scholars throughout history from trying to identify and connect him with others with the same name mentioned elsewhere. The

---

11. Wright, *The Early Christian Letters for Everyone, op. cit.,* 184.

140

name Gaius occurs five times in the New Testament, and likely refers to three different individuals:[12]

- Gaius who was immersed by Paul at Corinth (1 Cor. 1:14) and possibly also mentioned in Romans 16:23 as Paul's host while he wrote his letter to the Romans, and was a congregational leader.
- Gaius from Macedonia who accompanied Paul on his third emissary journey (Acts 19:29), and was seized along with Aristarchus during the Ephesian riot over Artemis in 56 C.E.
- Gaius of Derbe who traveled with Paul (Acts 20:4). According to a tradition recorded in the 4th century, Gaius of Derbe was appointed bishop of Pergamum by John the Apostle. This tradition also cites this particular Gaius as the recipient of 3 John *(Apostolic Constitutions 7.46.9)*.[13]

Although the above fourth century reference connects Gaius of Derbe with the recipient of the Third Epistle, the limited details about Gaius solely from 3 John render it nearly impossible to be absolutely certain of any conclusions or definite connections between him and those mentioned elsewhere.

What we can say with certainty, however, is that John and Gaius enjoyed a warm relationship, and that they were mutually bound together in love (vv. 1, 6) and truth (vv. 1, 3, 4, 8, 12). They were also part of an extended congregational network and affected by similar ecclesial politics.[14]

It is also likely that Gaius is Jewish, for two reasons: John uses the traditional Jewish circumlocution ("The Name") for God in verse 7, and in the same verse, he also differentiates his audience from "the Gentiles" (τῶν ἐθνικῶν - *ton ethnikon*). John is

---

12. Jobes, *op. cit.*, 289.
13. Ibid., 289.
14. Yarbrough, 363.

141

speaking to Gaius using "insider language." This letter obviously represents a period when the majority of followers of Yeshua were still predominantly Jewish and is not intended to be dismissive of "Messianic Gentiles" or meant to be derogatory.[15]

Jobes emphasizes that the opening verses introduce the author's primary concern, "the truth" (ἐν ἀληθείᾳ, *en alētheia*), which is mentioned four times in the first four verses.[16]

vv. 2-4 – Formal Greeting

---

2 Dear friend, I am praying that everything prosper with you and that you be in good health, as I know you are prospering spiritually. **3** For I was so happy when some brothers came and testified how faithful you are to the truth, as you continue living in the truth. **4** Nothing gives me greater joy than hearing that my children are living in the truth.

"Dear friend" - Marianne Meye Thompson points out the weakness of the English here: "While *dear friend* suggests cordiality, it is probably not strong enough to capture the meaning of the Greek word "beloved" (ἀγαπητῷ - *agapētō*) ... For love is not simply affection or attachment, but the God-given bond that unites [followers of Yeshua]."[17]

According to Craig S Keener, commenting on verse 2, "This is a standard greeting in many ancient letters, which quite often began with a prayer for the reader's health, frequently including the prayer that all would go well with the person (not just material prosperity, as some translations could be read as implying)."[18]

---

15. See Stern, *op. cit.*, 780.
16. Jobes, *op. cit.*, 286.
17. Thompson, *op. cit.*, 159.
18. Keener, *op. cit.*, 751.

Wright comments:

> As in the previous letter, John is delighted to know that someone is 'walking in the truth,' behaving with integrity which both reflects and embodies the truth of the gospel itself. We can take it that this involves not just correct doctrine and proper outward behavior, but that love for God and for one's fellow believers which, for John, is the sign that the truth of the gospel has really been grasped, not as an abstract idea but as what it is, the very life of God himself at work in his people.[19]

In verses 3-4, rabbis and philosophers often spoke of their disciples as their "children." John here is likely referring to those whom he had a direct role in leading to faith in Yeshua.[20] In later Jewish tradition, when someone converted to Judaism, the one responsible for overseeing their conversion was sometimes credited with "creating" the convert.[21]

vv. 5-8 – Gaius Commended for His Hospitality

5 Dear friend, you are faithful in all the work you are doing for the brothers, even when they are strangers to you. **6** They have testified to your love in front of the congregation. You will be doing well if you send them on their way in a manner worthy of God, **7** since it was for the sake of HaShem that they went out without accepting anything from the Gentiles. **8** It is we, therefore, who should support such people; so that we may share in their work for the truth.

---

19. Wright, *The Early Christian Letters for Everyone, op. cit.,* 184.
20. Keener, 751.
21. Ibid., 751.

Hospitality was a critical issue in the ancient world, and the Jewish community was especially concerned with taking care of its own. Most inns also served as brothels, or served as hosts to other unappealing dangers, so traveling Jews could expect to find hospitality from other Jews. And to prevent abuse of this system, these travelers would often carry letters of recommendation from someone the host might know to substantiate their character.

This practice became common among the followers of Yeshua, hence this personal letter from John.[22] Furthermore, the love he continually emphasizes, is that "which must then flow out into hospitality to fellow believers."[23] As Wright emphasizes, this love "was not something you did with your heart and emptions. It was something you did with your whole life, not least your money and your home. So it had been with Gaius."[24]

Thompson notes, "Gaius' generosity put into practice the admonition of 1 John 316-17 that [followers of Yeshua] give of their material possessions for each other."[25]

Wright adds:

> So common was this practice [of hosting travelers] that, not long after this letter was written, another early Christian writing, called 'The Teaching' (known as the *Didache*) had to lay down regulations for such travelers. 'Apostles' could stay at most two days, and ordinary [believers] a maximum of three. If generous love was to be the rule for the hosts, the guests needed clear boundaries so as not to abuse that love. As we see in 1 and 2 Thessalonians and 1 Timothy, the [believers] had to make clear that its obligation to care for one another was not the same thing as an invitation to lazy spongers.[26]

22. Ibid., 751.
23. Wright, *The Early Christian Letters for Everyone, op. cit.,* 184.
24. Ibid., 185.
25. Thompson, *op. cit.,* 160-161.
26. Wright, *The Early Christian Letters for Everyone, op. cit.,* 184-185.

Verse 7 states, *"it was for the sake of HaShem that they went out ..."* The Greek literally reads *"for the sake of the Name."* David Stern's use of HaShem accurately reflects the Greek, using what scholars now recognize as the typical Jewish circumlocution for the Name of God (the Tetragrammaton).[27] The term HaShem is used infrequently in the Tanakh (Lev. 24:11; Deut. 28:58), but very frequently in rabbinic texts.

Because 3 John is the only book in the New Testament that does not explicitly mention Yeshua, some have argued v.7's use of "The Name" was meant to refer to Yeshua (which is possible), but it is more likely that John was simply using a typical Jewish reference for God.

vv. 9-10 – Rebuke of Diotrephes

9 I wrote something to the congregation; but Diotrephes, who likes to be the macher among them, doesn't recognize our authority. **10** So if I come, I will bring up everything he is doing, including his spiteful and groundless gossip about us. And as if that weren't enough for him, he refuses to recognize the brothers' authority either; moreover, he stops those who want to do so and tries to drive them out of the congregation!

Diotrephes refused to show hospitality to those emissaries who had letters of recommendation from John, and refused to accept the authority of John which stood behind those emissaries. To reject a person's representative or those recommended by a person was to disrespect the person who wrote on their behalf.[28]

---

27. Jonathan Brumberg-Kraus. "The Third Letter of John," *The Jewish Annotated New Testament*, Ed. Amy-Jill Levine and Marc Zvi Brettler (New York: Oxford), 458.
28. Keener, *op. cit.,* 751.

Wright cautions concerning individuals like Diotrephes:

Part of the problem in any human dispute, in fact, is that only very rarely is one party completely and utterly in the right, and the other one completely and utterly in the wrong. It takes two to have a dispute, people say. That is not, actually, always the case: there really are some bullies out there, and one of the most damaging things they do is to make their victims imagine that they themselves are to blame. And yet judgements have to be made, decisions have to be taken, and not everyone is going to like them.[29]

As though Diotrephes' disrespect of John's authority were not enough, he also (v.10) spoke *lashon hara* (gossip) against John that was spiteful and groundless, and would not submit to others authority either.[30]

Diotrephes was not in submission to apostolic authority, and was not acting in ways consistent with what is scripturally expected of spiritual leaders. This is why John had to warn Gaius about Diotrephes.

Thompson contends: "Evidently the Elder and Diotrephes are engaged in a struggle for authority in the congregation to which Diotrephes belongs. That the Elder believes he has a right to challenge Diotrephes' power suggests that this congregation was founded by the Elder's efforts, either directly or indirectly."[31]

v. 11 – Closing Encouragement to Gaius

11 Dear friend, don't imitate the bad, but the good. Those who do what is good are from God; those who do what is bad are not from God.

---

29. Wright, *The Early Christian Letters for Everyone, op. cit.*, 188.
30. Stern, *op. cit.*, 780.
31. Thompson, *op. cit.*, 162.

In these closing words of encouragement to Gaius, John encourages him to avoid the influence of Diotrephes, and instructs Gaius, as Thompson notes, to imitate what is good:

> Good here is not a general category of 'good things,' but specifically the good that comes from God, that is in harmony with God's character and in keeping with God's actions. Above all, that good is good the good of love modeled and inspired by God. 'Let us love one another, for love is of God' (1 Jn 4:7; 3:10; 4:20). Love for others demonstrates both love for God and the indwelling love of God flowing through that person.[32]

v. 12– Recommendation of Demetrius

---

12 Everyone speaks well of Demetrius, and so does the truth itself. We vouch for him, and you know that our testimony is true.

Wright correctly notes the sharp contrast between the character of Diotrephes described above and that of Demetrius.[33]

No one in Diotrephes' congregation would welcome Demetrius, so John appeals to Gaius to help him and extend hospitality. John writes that Demetrius is spoken well of by everyone. According to Thomspon, "this translation is perhaps too weak. The Greek conveys the sense that Demetrius has faithful and true witnesses who will attest to his character. Even *the truth itself* joins in this testimony."[34]

---

32. Ibid., 163.
33. Wright, *The Early Christian Letters for Everyone, op. cit.,* 188.
34. Thompson, *op. cit.,* 164.

David Stern points out that according to early tradition, Peter ordained a man called Demetrius as a bishop in Philadelphia *(Apostolic Constitutions 7:46)*.[35]

vv. 13-14 – Closing

13 I have much to write you, but I don't want to write with pen and ink; **14** however, I am hoping to see you very soon, and we will speak face to face. Shalom to you. Your friends send you their greetings. Greet each of our friends by name.

"Paper" is of course a reference to papyrus, made from reeds and rolled up like a scroll. The pen was a reed sharpened to a point at the end, and the ink was a compound of charcoal, vegetable gum and water.[36] According to Keener: "Written letters were considered an inferior substitution for personal presence or for a speech, and writers sometimes concluded their letters with the promise to discuss matters further face-to-face."[37]

Regarding the latter half of verse 14, Keener comments, "Greetings were an essential part of the social protocol at the time, and the greeting ([*Shalom aleichem*] *'Peace be upon you'*) was intended as a blessing or prayer to impart peace.[38]

Conclusion

John's third letter may seem short and insignificant, but it actually has much to say. It has lessons in leadership and character,

---

35. Stern, *op. cit.*, 780.
36. Keener, *op. cit.*, 749.
37. Ibid., 749.
38. Ibid., 749.

and what true *faith in action* looks like, specifically in regard to hospitality.

In this letter we learn that hospitality is far more than cordiality or pleasantries. Rather, care for one another is an embodiment of Yeshua's command to love God and love one another (Matthew 22:37-40).

Another matter addressed is authority and trustworthiness. When one who carries the recommendation of others, they are to be trusted (unless proven otherwise). This is why the ordination[39] of clergy is so important, especially traditional ordination which requires the recognition and transmission of authority from others. Within both historic Jewish and Christian tradition there is no such thing as self-ordination. Of course one's authority ultimately comes from God through the Spirit, but equally along with that must be the recognition of other leaders. Otherwise, we run the risk of becoming like Diotrephes, and thinking of ourselves more highly than we ought. When one has been ordained, not only is authority to interpret Scripture and the authority to lead and teach transmitted onto a person, but the ordination also carries a recommendation from the ordaining authorities. It tells others that the one ordained was discipled and raised-up and has been recognized and entrusted as a spiritual leader.

Within Judaism ordination is described as 'Mosaic succession,' meaning the authority of Moses is passed down to succeeding generations through the laying on of hands (סמיכה, *s'mikhah*). In historic Christianity, this is embodied in the concept of Apostolic Succession, where the authority of the original apostles was transmitted to succeeding generations also through the laying on

---

39. Ordination is the process by which individuals are consecrated, that is, set apart as clergy to perform various religious rites and ceremonies. The process and ceremonies of ordination vary by religion and denomination.

of hands. Within both historic traditions, the one ordained has spiritual authority because they received it from those who were before them, going (theoretically) all the way back to either Moses and/or the apostles. It is a spiritual chain linking each generation together.

Obviously, ordination alone does not always guarantee sound theology or behavior, but it at least demonstrates a level of accountability and preparation that self-recognition does not. That is also why there is greater reliability. In Demetrius' case, he comes with a letter of recommendation from the apostle John himself, telling Gaius that Demetrius can be trusted even though they had never previously met.

Reflection Questions

1. Why was hospitality such an important issue for the early believing community?

2. How is caring for one another an embodiment of Yeshua's command to love God and love one another (Mt. 22:36-40)?

3. Do you think Diotrephes receives fair treatment in the letter?

4. If you were Gaius, would you welcome and support Demetrius based only on a letter of recommendation from John?

5. Why do you think this short book was included in the canon of the New Testament, especially since Yeshua is not specifically mentioned?

6. Is this book still relevant today, and if so, why and how?

7.

CONCLUSION

The Letters of John offer us a window into the earliest circles of Yeshua-followers, when the original apostles were still influential leaders and the movement's adherents were still primarily Jewish (although this was rapidly changing). It is important to emphasize that when we speak of John's Judaism, it is time-bound. It is not a variety of a timeless Judaism, but of Second Temple Judaism. The Jewish context and thought described in John's letters is not the Judaism we are all familiar with today (although it is related). The Jewish world of the New Testament is pre-rabbinic, yet reveals an important link in the development of Judaism leading into the rabbinic period.

John wrote his letters to confront a split over conflicting theologies and behavioral concerns. Certain individuals broke away from the network of congregations under John's care and authority and were traveling around attempting to influence others with their false teachings. John's primary concern was to both encourage and warn all those who looked to him for guidance.

Although John wrote to address these particular pastoral concerns, he also wrote to provide hope, encouragement, and guidance. His letters also provide significant contributions on a number of key theological issues and themes which remain relevant to the present day. First and foremost is John's hermeneutic for interpreting everything in Scripture: our love for God and our love for one another. This understanding must always influence the way we read and interpret John's writings.

Furthermore, John reminds us to live *now* for the return of Messiah. Our theologies should shape our interactions with the world, one another, and with God. Every day we should be expecting the return of Messiah … in thought and in deed. This is why John emphasizes observance and the importance of community. Our lives are intimately linked together, and false teaching and improper behavior are dangerous because they affect all of us. That is why we must remain focused and committed to one another and producing spiritual fruit.[1]

We also learned from John that hospitality is far more than cordiality or pleasantries. Rather, care for one another is an embodiment of Yeshua's command to love God and love one another (Matthew 22:37-40).

Another matter addressed is authority and trustworthiness. A person who carries the recommendation of others is to be trusted (unless proven otherwise). This is why the ordination[2] of clergy is so important, especially traditional ordination which requires the recognition and transmission of authority from others. Of course one's authority ultimately comes from God through the Spirit, but equally along with that must be the recognition of other leaders. When one has been ordained or officially recognized, not only is authority to interpret Scripture and the authority to lead

---

1. Galatians 5:22-23
2. Ordination is the process by which individuals are consecrated, that is, set apart as clergy to perform various religious rites and ceremonies. The process and ceremonies of ordination vary by religion and denomination.

and teach transmitted to a person, but the ordination also carries a recommendation from the ordaining authorities. It tells others that the one ordained was discipled and raised-up and has been recognized and entrusted as a spiritual leader.

John's letters include some of the most beloved and often-quoted portions of scripture. Countless sermons have been given on their verses and they are intimately familiar to innumerable individuals across time. May John's message of hope, love and covenant fidelity continue to inspire you and countless generations to come until the Messiah returns *(May it be soon!)*.

Although I have much to write you people, I would rather not use paper and ink. Instead, I hope to come and see you and to talk with you face to face, so that our joy may be complete. (2 John 1:12)

GLOSSARY

This glossary contains certain words, phrases, concepts, and individuals that are regularly referred to within biblical and theological studies, but which some readers may not already be familiar with.

1 Clement – Traditionally attributed to Clement of Rome, it is a letter addressed to the followers of Yeshua in the city of Corinth. The letter dates from the late 1st or early 2nd century, and considered one of the earliest extant Christian documents (along with the Didache) outside of the canonical New Testament.

ADONAI – Literally, "My Lord," a Hebrew word used by Jews to represent the Tetragrammaton, the sacred name of God consisting of the four Hebrew letters *Yud-Hey-Vav-Hey*. Usually rendered in English bibles as LORD (all capital letters).

Aggadah – From the Aramaic, "to tell," refers to homiletic stories used to make a point, illustrate an idea, or clarify a problem.

Apocrypha – The term comes from the Greek word meaning "hidden" or "secret" and refers to biblical books included in the Septuagint and Vulgate but excluded from Jewish and Protestant canons.

Apocalypse – The term Ἀποκάλυψις *(apocalypsis)* is a Greek word meaning "revelation", an unveiling or unfolding of things previously hidden. As a genre, apocalyptic literature details the authors' visions of the end times as often revealed through a heavenly messenger or Angel.

155

Apocalyptic – A genre of prophetic writing that developed in post-Exilic Jewish culture, beginning around the third-century B.C.E. The apocalyptic literature of Judaism and Christianity embraces a considerable period, from the centuries following the Babylonian exile to the close of the Middle Ages.

Barnabas – A non-canonical Greek epistle preserved complete in the 4th century Codex Sinaiticus where it appears at the end of the New Testament.

B.C.E./C.E. – The abbreviations B.C.E. and C.E., which mean "Before the Common Era" and "Common Era," are commonly used among scholars, and within the Jewish community, instead of the more common B.C. ("Before Christ") and A.D. (*"Anno Domini"* which is Latin for "in the year of our Lord").

Canon (Canonical) – From the Greek κανών, meaning "rule" or "measuring stick," and refers to those biblical books that are considered the most authoritative regarding matters of faith, theology and doctrine.

Chassidic/Chassidut/Chassidim – *Chassidut* (חסידות) is a mystical form of Judaism that birthed out of a revival movement that arose in Western Ukraine during the 18th century and spread rapidly across Eastern Europe. It was founded by Rabbi Israel Ben Eliezer, commonly known as the "Ball Shem Tov," and his followers were called "Chassidim." Today there are various groups, and the greatest number of Chassidim live in the United States and Israel. It has had a tremendous impact on the development of modern Judaism (even for those who are not Chassidic).

Codex Alexandrinus – A 5th century manuscript of one of the three earliest and most important manuscripts of the Bible in Greek, containing the majority of the Septuagint and the New Testament. Along with the Codex Sinaiticus and the Vaticanus it is one of the earliest and most complete manuscripts of the Bible.

156

Codex Sinaiticus – A mid-4th century handwritten copy of the Greek Bible containing the oldest complete copy of the New Testament. Along with the Codex Alexandrinus and the Vaticanus, it is one of the three most important manuscripts of the Bible and considered a celebrated historical treasure.

Codex Vaticanus – One of the oldest extant manuscripts of the Greek Bible (4th century). It is named after its place of conservation in the Vatican Library, where it has been kept since at least the 15th century. Along with the Codex Alexandrinus and the Sinaiticus, it is one of the three most important copies of the Bible.

Dead Sea Scrolls – A collection of manuscripts discovered between 1946 and 1956 at Khirbet Qumran. The texts were found inside caves about a mile inland from the northwest shore of the Dead Sea, from which they derive their name. They are considered the most important archaeological find in relation to biblical studies and our understanding of the Second Temple period.

Deuterocanonical – Regarding the books of Scripture contained in the Septuagint but not in the Hebrew and Protestant canons, also known as apocryphal books.

Dibbur – The Hebrew word *dibbur* (דִּיבּוּר) means "word" or "speak" but is often used hypostatically within midrash as a reference to God's spoken Word. For more, please see the section in the Introduction, *The Thoroughly Jewish Context of John's Theology*.

Dionysius of Alexandria – Dionysius was a 3rd century bishop. He studied under Origen and Heraclas in Alexandria, and succeeded Heraclas as the head of the catechetical school in 231. Dionysius became the bishop of Alexandria in 248. His correspondence survives primarily through quotations from Eusebius.

Doxology - The term derives from the Greek word δοξολογία *(doxologia)*, meaning "glory." It refers to a short hymn of praise often added to the end of certain New Testament books and liturgical psalms and hymns. The practice is believed to derive

157

from synagogue liturgy, where versions of the *Kaddish* are used to conclude particular sections of the service. Within Christian liturgical traditions the doxology has largely evolved into meaning only the closing hymn at the end of the service.

Ephesus – (Greek: Ἔφεσος) was an ancient Greek seaport on the Western coast of modern-day Turkey. It was the city where Paul wrote his epistle (Ephesians) and where the Apostle John eventually settled around the time the Temple in Jerusalem was destroyed (c.70 C.E.), and where it is believed he composed his gospel and letters.

Eschatology – Various understandings, discussions or allusions to the End of the Word, the Second Coming, the resurrection of the dead, or the Final Judgment.

Eusebius – Eusebius of Caesarea (263-339), also known as Eusebius Pamphili, was a historian of Christianity, exegete, and polemicist. He became the bishop of Caesarea Maritima around 314 C.E. He was a scholar of the Biblical canon and is regarded as one of the most important figures within Christian history.

Fiscus Iudaicus – A unique Roman tax Jews were forced to pay due to their refusal to participate in the Imperial cult. The Imperial cult identified Roman emperors as divinely sanctioned authorities, and along with its various expected rituals, was inseparable from the worship of Rome's official deities. Jews, and later Christians, found this idea offensive and refused to participate in the veneration.

Gamatria – Numerology based on the Hebrew letters. In Hebrew, letters also have a numerical value.

Gnosticism – From the Greek word, *gnôsis*, meaning "knowledge" or "insight." It is the term used for a loosely organized religious and philosophical movement that flourished in the first and second centuries C.E. This heresy taught a dualism between a supreme deity and a semi-divine, and lesser-deity, known as the *Demiurge, who is associated with the material, physical world.* To overcome the material world and rise to the Supreme God, the Gnostic must do so

158

through secret knowledge, which mixed philosophy, metaphysics, curiosity, culture, knowledge, and the secrets of history and the universe.

God-fearers – In Greek: φοβούμενος τὸν Θεόν - *Phoboumenos ton Theon*. This is a technical term referring to a numerous class of Gentiles who affiliated with synagogues and took on certain Jewish observances and traditions without becoming full converts to Judaism. They existed even before the spread of the Gospel message. God-fearers are regularly mentioned throughout the New Testament, and included individuals of significant social standing (like Cornelius in Acts 10). References to God-fearers are also found in synagogue inscriptions and in ancient literature (Greek, Roman, and Jewish). Specific citations in the New Testament include: Acts 13:16; 13:26; 13:49; 17:4; 17:17; 18:7.

Halakhah – The Hebrew word (הלכה) literally means "the way to walk," and refers to the instruction and application of Jewish law.

Hanukkah – Also known as the "Feast of Dedication," celebrates the re-dedication of the Temple in Jerusalem following the victory of the Maccabees over the Syrian-Greek army in the 2nd century B.C.E. The holiday is also relevant to followers of Yeshua, for according to John 10:22-39, Yeshua also observed Hanukkah.

Hermeneutic(s) – The theory, methodology and discipline of interpretation, especially the interpretation of biblical texts.

Hoshanah Rabbah – in Hebrew, means "the Great Hosanna," and is the seventh day of the biblical festival of Sukkot (John 7:37-44). Additional prayers of thanksgiving are added to the daily prayers, and during the Second Temple period, included a joyous water drawing ceremony called the *Simchat Beit HaSho'evah*, in which water was drawn from the Pool of Siloam and then joyously paraded up to the temple mount to be used for pouring over the special holiday sacrifices.

Irenaeus – Born around 125 C.E., as a young man in Smyrna (near Ephesus, in what is now western Turkey) he heard the preaching of Polycarp, who as a young man had heard the teaching of the Apostle John. Afterward, probably while still a young man, Polycarp moved west to Lyons in southern France. In 177 Irenaeus was appointed Bishop of Lyons following a severe persecution in the city which claimed the lives of the previous bishop and others. He died around 202 C.E. He is thus an important link between the apostles and later times, and also an important link between Eastern and Western Christianity.

Jerusalem Council – An early guiding body convened around 50/51 C.E. made up of the Apostles (Emissaries), Elders, and other prominent figures within the Yeshua-believing community. The purpose of the council, according to Acts 15 and Galatians 2, was to decide whether or not Gentiles must convert to Judaism and, therefore, be obligated to observe all the commandments of the Torah. The final decision, after much debate, was that Gentiles are not required to convert, and therefore, are not obligated to keep most of the commandments. However, they did retain the prohibitions against idolatry, fornication, eating blood, and meat not properly slaughtered (i.e. "strangled," in most English versions) (see Acts 15:10-11 and 19-29).

Kaddish – The Hebrew word *kaddish* (קדיש) is a variation of the root "holy" and refers to a hymn of praise to God found throughout the Jewish prayer service. The central theme of the Kaddish is the magnification and sanctification of God's name. Various versions of the Kaddish are used to conclude particular sections of the service.

Kavanah – The Hebrew word *kavanah* (כונה) means focus, intention, or meaning. It is the filter through which our observance flows out.

Logos – The Geek word *logos* [λόγος] can variously mean "word", "speech", "reason", and "discourse" but is often used hypostatically as a reference to God's spoken Word. For more on this, please refer to the section in the Introduction, *The Thoroughly Jewish Context of John's Theology* and the commentary to 1 John 1.

Masoretic Text – Often abbreviated as MT, the Masoretic Text is the authoritative Hebrew (with some Aramaic) version of the 24 books of the Tanakh for Rabbinic Judaism. It is called the Masoretic Text because it is based on the textual tradition of Jewish scholars known as the *Masoretes*. The Masoretes meticulously assembled and codified, and supplied the text with diacritical marks to enable correct pronunciation. They also divided each book into sections and verses, separated the apocryphal from the canonical books, and divided the latter into twenty-two books, being the number of letters in the Hebrew alphabet. This monumental work was begun around the 6th century C.E. and completed in the 10th.

Memra – The Aramaic memra (מֶמְרָא) is often used hypostatically in Aramaic texts as a reference to God's spoken Word. For more on this, please see the section in the Introduction, *The Thoroughly Jewish Context of John's Theology* and the commentary to 1 John 1.

Midrash – an interpretive method and creative body of literature which seeks to "fill-in the gaps" and answer questions within Scripture. It does so through delving into the deeper meaning of words, finding similarities with other biblical passages, and using Hebrew word plays, numerology and parables.

Mishnah – The word "Mishnah" comes from the Hebrew root *sha'nah* (שנה), and literally means "to repeat [what one was taught]" and is often used as "to learn". It was codified in Israel around 200 C.E. by Yehudah HaNassi. The Mishnah is a "teaching text," a curriculum of Jewish learning meant to be studies with a teacher. The Mishnah is divided into Six Orders, each dealing with a broad area of Jewish life.

Mitzvah (plural: *Mitzvot*) – Specifically refers to the commands of the Torah. However, the word is also often used to refer to a moral deed performed as a religious duty – as an extension of the *mitzvot*.

Nasi – A term regularly used throughout the Hebrew Bible which is often translated as "prince" or "captain." During the Second Temple period (c. 530 B.C.E. – 70 C.E.) the term was used for the highest ranking member of the Sanhedrin (the great assembly of sages).

161

Papias – an early Apostolic Father and Bishop of Hierapolis (now in Turkey), who lived c. 60–163 C.E. His work "Explanation of the Sayings of the Lord" is now extant only in fragments, but provides important apostolic oral source accounts of the history of primitive Christianity and of the origins of the Gospels. According to the 2nd-century theologian Irenaeus, Papias had known the Apostle John. The 4th-century historian Eusebius of Caesarea critically records that Papias derived his material not only from John the Evangelist but also from John the Presbyter. Papias' interpretation of the Gospels was used by Eastern and Western Christian theologians down to the early 4th century.

Pesher (Pesharim) – A specific type of interpretive (midrashic) literature known from the Dead Sea Scrolls, which is a collection of manuscripts discovered between 1946 and 1956 at *Khirbet Qumran*. The texts were found inside caves about a mile inland from the northwest shore of the Dead Sea, from which they derive their name.

Philo (Philo Judaeus) – Also known as Philo of Alexandria (c. 20 B.C.E. – 50 C.E.), was a Hellenistic Jewish philosopher who lived in Alexandria, in the Roman province of Egypt. He used philosophical allegory to harmonize Jewish scripture with Greek philosophy. His methodology blended both Jewish exegesis and Stoic philosophy. Although his allegorical exegesis was important for several early Christian Church Fathers, his work had little influence within later Rabbinic Judaism. Philo believed that literal interpretations of the Hebrew Bible would stifle humanity's perception of a God too complex and marvelous to be understood in literal human terms.

Polycarp – Born around 69 C.E. and died around 156 C.E. (at the age of 86 or 87). Along with Clement of Rome and Ignatius of Antioch, Polycarp is considered as one of three chief Apostolic Fathers. Both Irenaeus (who as a young man heard Polycarp speak) and Tertullian recorded that Polycarp had been a disciple of John the Apostle. Jerome wrote that Polycarp was a disciple of John and that John had ordained him bishop of Smyrna. According to the

Martyrdom of Polycarp he died a martyr, bound and burned at the stake, then stabbed when the fire failed to touch him.

Interestingly, it is recorded that Polycarp continued to advocate for the observance of Easter during Passover. According to Irenaeus he visited Rome to discuss the differences that existed between Asia and Rome "with regard to certain things" and especially about the time of Easter. On certain things the two bishops speedily came to an understanding, while regarding Easter, each adhered to his own custom, without breaking off communion with the other. Polycarp followed the eastern practice of celebrating the feast on the 14th of Nissan, the day of Passover. Anicetus (bishop of Rome) followed the western practice of celebrating the feast on the first Sunday after the first full moon after the Spring equinox.

Pseudepigrapha – A genre of non-canonical writings which became especially popular between 200 B.C.E. and 200 C.E. (and even later). This body of literature claims to have been written by biblical figures and prophets, but was actually written by anonymous authors, and often at a much later time in history than the ascribed figures lived.

RaMbaM – An acronym for "Rabbi Moshe ben Maimon," also known as Maimonides (b.1135 in Cordoba, Spain and d.1204 in Fustat, Egypt). He was a Sephardic Jewish philosopher and physician, and one of the most prolific and influential Torah commentators of the Middle Ages. He was buried in Tiberias, Israel.

Sanhedrin – The council of seventy-one Jewish sages who constituted the Supreme Court and legislative body in Judea during the Roman period.

Semitism – A linguistic term for a characteristic feature of a Semitic language that occurs in another language. This includes the use of certain vocabulary, style and/or syntax influenced by, or borrowed from Hebrew and Aramaic. The most common examples are texts written in Jewish Koine Greek.

Septuagint – Commonly abbreviated as simply LXX, is the earliest Greek translation of the Hebrew Bible (Old Testament) dating to the 3rd and 2nd centuries B.C.E.

Shepherd of Hermas – A 2nd century work considered canonical scripture by some of the early Church fathers. It had great authority in the 2nd and 3rd centuries.

Sukkot – The Feast of Tabernacles is a biblical eight day commemoration of the Israelites' wandering in the desert for forty years (Leviticus 23:33-44; Numbers 29:12-39; Deut. 16:13-17; etc.). During those years, they did not have a permanent place to live and had to live in temporary shelters *(sukkot)*. Therefore, every year, during Sukkot, we are commanded to continue dwelling in temporary shelters to remind us of the temporal nature of our lives (Lev. 23:42-43). Another central practice is the waiving of the *Lulav* and *Etrog* (Lev. 23:40) during the recitation of *Hallel*, which are special prayers of thanksgiving recited on holidays. Sukkot reminds us that everything we have in life is from God, and to be thankful for everything God provides.

Synoptic Gospels – The term synoptic comes from the Greek σύνοψις, synopsis, i.e. "seeing all together, synopsis." The gospels of Matthew, Mark, and Luke are referred to as the Synoptic Gospels because they include many of the same stories, often in a similar sequence and in similar or sometimes identical wording. They stand in contrast to John, whose content is comparatively distinct.

Targum – תרגום (plural = תרגומים, *targumim*) literally means "translation" and is an ancient Aramaic paraphrase or interpretation of the Hebrew Bible. They were not just translations, but included interpretation and commentary. They emerged in the first century C.E. when Hebrew was declining as a spoken language. Often in synagogues a passage would first be read in Hebrew and then a Targum would be read (or recited). The most famous Targumim include *Onkelos* and *Jonathan*.

Tertullian – Was born c.155 or 160 C.E. in Carthage (now in Tunisia) and died after 220 C.E. He was an important early theologian, polemicist, and moralist who, as the initiator of ecclesiastical Latin, was instrumental in shaping the vocabulary and thought of Western Christianity.

Testament of the Twelve Patriarchs – A pseudepigraphic work containing the dying commands of the twelve sons of Jacob. The Testaments were written in Hebrew or Greek, and reached their final form in the 2nd century C.E. Fragments of similar writings were found at Qumran, but scholars are divided as to whether these are the same texts. It is considered apocalyptic literature.

Torah – The word literally means "teaching" or "instruction." It specifically refers to the first five books of the Bible – Genesis, Exodus, Leviticus, Numbers and Deuteronomy. However, it can also be used to refer to Jewish teaching more generally.

Tanakh – Jews refer to the Scriptures as the Tanakh (תנ"ך), which is an acronym for the three primary sections of the Hebrew Bible – the *Torah* (Pentateuch), *Neviim* (Prophets) and *Khetuvim* (Writings). The canon of the Christian Old Testament includes the same books as the Jewish canon, but arranged in a different order.

Yeshua – The earliest followers of Jesus knew him by his original Hebrew name, Yeshua (ישוע), the masculine form of the word for Salvation/Redemption, ישועה).

BIBLIOGRAPHY

Allen, David L. *1-3 John*. Preaching the Word commentary series, Wheaton: Crossway, 2013.

Ancient History Encyclopedia. "The Great Jewish Revolt of 66 C.E." Accessed March 3, 2019 - https://www.ancient.eu/article/823/the-great-jewish-revolt-of-66-C.E./

Bauckham, Richard. *Gospel of Glory*. Grand Rapids: Baker Academic, 2015.

_____. *Jesus and the God of Israel*. Grand Rapids: William B. Eerdmans, 2009.

_____. *The Testimony of the Beloved Disciple*. Grand Rapids: Baker Academic, 2007.

Boyarin, Daniel. *Borderlines: The Partition of Judaeo-Christianity*. Philadelphia: University of Pennsylvania Press, 2004.

_____. "Logos, A Jewish Word: John's Prologue as Midrash." *The Jewish Annotated New Testament*, Ed. Amy-Jill Levine and Marc Zvi Brettler. New York: Oxford, 2011.

_____. *The Jewish Gospels*. New York: The New Press, 2012.

Bruce, F.F. *The Book of Acts*. The New International Commentary on the New Testament, Grand Rapids: Wm. B. Eerdmans, 1988.

Brumbach, Joshua. *Jude: On Faith and the Destructive Influence of Heresy*. Clarksville: Lederer, 2014.

Brumberg-Kraus, Jonathan. "The Third Letter of John." *The Jewish Annotated New Testament*, Ed. Amy-Jill Levine and Marc Zvi Brettler. New York: Oxford, 2011.

Buber, Martin. *Ten Rungs: Hasidic Sayings*. New York: Schocken Books, 1973.

Charlesworth, James H. Ed. *Jesus' Jewishness*. New York: Crossroad, 1997.

Collins, Adela Yarbro and John J. *King and Messiah as Son of God*. Eerdmans Publishing, 2008.

Complete Jewish Study Bible. Peabody: Hendrickson, 2016.

Dosick, Wayne. *Living Judaism*. New York: Harper Collins, 1995.

Eusebius, *Ecclesiastical History*. Grand Rapids: Baker, 1976.

Fields, Harvey J. *A Torah Commentary for Our Times: Vol. III*. New York: UAHC Press, 1993.

Flusser, David. *The Sage from Galilee*. Grand Rapids: Eerdmans Publishing, 2007.

Galambush, Julie. "The Second Letter of John," *The Jewish Annotated New Testament*, Ed. Amy-Jill Levine and Marc Zvi Brettler. New York: Oxford, 2011.

Hakola, Raimo. "The Johannine Community as Jewish Christians? Some Problems in Current Scholarly Consensus." *Jewish Christianity Reconsidered*. Ed. Matt Jackson-McCabe. Minneapolis: Fortress Press, 2007.

Hurtado, Larry W. *How on Earth did Jesus Become a God?* Grand Rapids: William B. Eerdmans, 2005.

_____. *One God, One Lord: Early Christian Devotion and Ancient Jewish Monotheism*. Philadelphia: Fortress Press, 1998.

Jobes, Karen H. *1, 2, & 3 John*. Zondervan Exegetical Commentary on the New Testament, 19, Grand Rapids: Zondervan, 2014.

Johnson, Thomas F. *1, 2 & 3 John*. Understanding the Bible Commentary Series, Grand Rapids: Baker Books, 1993.

Keener, Craig S. *The IVP Bible Background Commentary: New Testament*. Downers Grove: IVP Academic, 1993.

Kinbar, Carl. Addendum to "Israel, Interpretation, and the Knowledge of God." A paper presented at the 2010 Hashivenu forum, Agoura Hills, CA.

Kinzer, Mark S. "Israel's Eschatological Renewal in Water and Spirit: A Messianic Jewish Perspective on Baptism." Paper prepared for the 2009 Messianic Jewish – Roman Catholic Dialogue Group (September 2009).

_____. *Israel's Messiah and the People of God*. Ed. Jennifer M. Rosner. Eugene: Cascade Press, 2011.

Kraftchick, Steven J. *Jude, 2 Peter*. Abingdon New Testament Commentaries, Nashville: Abingdon Press, 2002.

Kruse, Colin G. *The Letters of John*. The Pillar New Testament Commentary, Grand Rapids: Eerdmans, 2000.

Lancaster, D. Thomas. *Holy Epistle to the Galatians*. Marshfield: First Fruits of Zion, 2011.

_____. *Torah Club: Chronicles of the Messiah,* Vol. 6. Marshfield: First Fruits of Zion, 2011.

Levertoff, Paul Philip. *Love and the Messianic Age*. Marshfield: Vine of David, 2009.

Levine, Amy-Jill. *The Misunderstood Jew*. New York: Harper Collins, 2006.

_____ and Marc Zvi Brettler*, Eds. The Jewish Annotated New Testament*. New York: Oxford, 2011.

Lichtenstein, Yechiel Tzvi. *Sugiyot Nivcharot B'sefer HaBrit HaChadashah*. Jerusalem: Keren Ahavah Meshichit, 2002.

Lizorkin-Eyzenberg, Eli. *The Jewish Gospel of John*. Tel Mond: Israel Study Center, 2015.

Miller, John W. *How the Bible Came to Be*. New York: Paulist Press, 2004.

Murray, Michele. "The First Letter of John," *The Jewish Annotated New Testament*, Ed. Amy-Jill Levine and Marc Zvi Brettler. New York: Oxford, 2011.

Nanos, Mark D. *The Mystery of Romans*. Minneapolis: Fortress Press, 1996.

Ronning, John. *The Jewish Targums and John's Logos Theology*. Peabody: Hendrickson, 2010.

Sacks, Jonathan. *The Koren Rosh HaShanah Machzor*. Jerusalem: Koren Publishers, 2011.

Shanks, Hershel. *The Mystery and Meaning of the Dead Sea Scrolls*. New York: Random House, 1998.

Stern, David H. *Complete Jewish Bible*. Clarksville: Jewish New Testament Publications, 1998.

_____. *Jewish New Testament Commentary*. Clarksville: Jewish New Testament Publications, 1992.

Stott, John R. W. *The Epistles of John*. Tyndale New Testament Commentaries, Grand Rapids: Wm. B. Eerdmans, 1978.

Strong's Concordance of the Bible. Accessed via biblehub.com (March 30, 2019) - https://biblehub.com/greek/225.htm

The Holy Bible: English Standard Version. Wheaton: Crossway, 2002.

Thompson, Marianne Meye. *1-3 John.* The IVP New Testament Commentary Series, 19, Downers Grove: IVP Academic, 1992.

Tomson, Peter J. *'If This Be From Heaven...'* Sheffield: Sheffield Academic Press, 2001.

Vermes, Geza. *Jesus the Jew.* Minneapolis: Fortress Press, 1981.

Wright, N.T. *The Early Christian Letters for Everyone.* New Testament for Everyone, Louisville: Westminster John Knox, 2011.

_____. *The Letters of John.* N.T. Wright for Everyone Bible Study Guides, Downers Grove: Intervarsity Press, 2012.

Yarbrough, Robert W. *1-3 John.* Baker Exegetical Commentary on the New Testament, Grand Rapids: Baker Academic, 2008.

ABOUT THE AUTHOR

Joshua Brumbach is the Senior Rabbi of Beth Emunah Messianic Synagogue in Agoura Hills, California, adjunct instructor of Jewish Studies at Messianic Jewish Theological Institute (MJTI), and the author of a previous commentary in this series, *Jude: On Faith and the Destructive Influence of Heresy* (April 2014).

He is an accredited Jewish educator, has studied in various Jewish institutions including an Orthodox yeshiva in Europe, and is ordained by the Union of Messianic Jewish Congregations and the Messianic Jewish Rabbinical Council. He is currently completing a doctorate in Jewish Studies at Spertus, holds a MA in Rabbinic Writings from MJTI, a BA in Ancient Near Eastern Civilizations and Biblical Studies from UCLA, and an AA in Anthropology from Mt. Hood Community College.

Rabbi Joshua additionally serves as Vice-President of the Messianic Jewish Rabbinical Council, on several committees, including the Theology Committee, of the Union of Messianic Jewish Congregations, and on the Administration Committee for the International Messianic Jewish Alliance.

He is an avid mountain biker, loves the outdoors, is married to Monique, the Executive Director of the UMJC, and they have an elementary-age son.

First Time in History!

General Editor: Rabbi Barry Rubin
Theological Editor: Dr. John Fischer

The Complete Jewish Study Bible

Insights for Jews and Christians
—Dr. David H. Stern

A One-of-a-Kind Study Bible that illuminates the Jewish background and context of God's word so it is more fully understandable. Uses the updated *Complete Jewish Bible* text by David H. Stern, including notes from the *Jewish New Testament Commentary* and contributions from Scholars listed below. 1990 pages.

< Hardcover Edition

Hardback	978-1619708679	$49.95
Flexisoft	978-1619708693	$79.95
Leather	978-1619708709	$139.95

Leather Edition w/color gift box   Flexisoft Edition w/color sleeve

CONTRIBUTORS & SCHOLARS

Rabbi Dr. Glenn Blank	Forbes	Rabbi Barney Kasdan	Rosenberg
Dr. Michael Brown	Rabbi Dr. David	Dr. Craig S. Keener	Rabbi Isaac Roussel
Rabbi Steven Bernstein	Friedman	Rabbi Elliot Klayman	Dr. Michael Rydelnik
Rabbi Joshua	Dr. Arnold	Jordan Gayle Levy	Dr. Jeffrey Seif
Brumbach	Fruchtenbaum	Dr. Ronald Moseley	Rabbi Tzahi Shapira
Rabbi Ron Corbett	Dr. John Garr	Rabbi Dr. Rich Nichol	Dr. David H. Stern
Pastor Ralph Finley	Pastor David Harris	Rabbi Mark J. Rantz	Dr. Bruce Stokes
Rabbi Dr. John Fischer	Benjamin Juster	Rabbi Russ Resnik	Dr. Tom Tribelhorn
Dr. Patrice Fischer	Rabbi Dr. Daniel Juster	Dr. Richard Robinson	Dr. Forrest Weiland
Rebbitzen Malkah	Dr. Walter C. Kaiser	Rabbi Dr. Jacob	Dr. Marvin Wilson

QUOTES BY JEWISH SCHOLARS & SAGES

Dr. Daniel Boyarin
Dr. Amy-Jill Levine
Rabbi Jonathan Sacks
Rabbi Gamaliel
Rabbi Hillel
Rabbi Shammai
Rabbi Akiva
Maimonides
and many more

Complete Jewish Bible: *An English Version*

—Dr. David H. Stern (Available March 2017)

Now, the most widely used Messianic Jewish Bible around the world, has updated text with introductions added to each book, written from a biblically Jewish perspective. The CJB is a unified Jewish book, a version for Jews and non-Jews alike; to connect Jews with the Jewishness of the Messiah, and non-Jews with their Jewish roots. Names and terms are returned to their original Hebrew and presented in easy-to-understand transliterations, enabling the reader to say them the way *Yeshua* (Jesus) did! 1728 pages.

Paperback	978-1936716845	$29.95
Hardcover	978-1936716852	$34.95
Flexisoft Cover	978-1936716869	$49.95

Jewish New Testament
—Dr. David H. Stern

The New Testament is a Jewish book, written by Jews, initially for Jews. Its central figure was a Jew. His followers were all Jews; yet no other version really communicates its original, essential Jewishness. Uses neutral terms and Hebrew names. Highlights Jewish references and corrects mistranslations. Freshly translated into English from Greek, this is a must read to learn about first-century faith. 436 pages

Hardback	978-9653590069	**JB02**	$19.99
Paperback	978-9653590038	**JB01**	$14.99
Spanish	978-1936716272	**JB17**	$24.99

Also available in French, German, Polish, Portuguese and Russian.

Jewish New Testament Commentary
—Dr. David H. Stern

This companion to the *Jewish New Testament* enhances Bible study. Passages and expressions are explained in their original cultural context. 15 years of research. 960 pages.

Hardback	978-9653590083	**JB06**	$34.99
Paperback	978-9653590113	**JB10**	$29.99

Is Christ *Really* The "End of The Law"?
Another Look at *Telos* in Romans 10:4
—Drs. Jeffrey and Barri Cae Seif

"There are few Pauline statements more controversial than Romans 10:4, specifically the meaning of the word τέλος, telos.

τέλος γὰρ νόμου Χριστὸς εἰς δικαιοσύνην παντὶ τῷ πιστεύοντι.

The verse has traditionally been rendered, "For Christ is the *end* of the Law for righteousness to everyone who believes." Some say, "For the *goal* at which the Torah aims is the Messiah" while others prefer *new beginning*. Still others offer, "For Messiah is the *end* of the Torah, that everyone who has faith may be justified" or "Messiah is the *culmination* of the Torah so that there may be righteousness for everyone believes." 179 Pages

Paperback	978-1733935418	$21.99

Messianic Jewish Orthodoxy
The Essence of Our Faith, History and Best Practices
–Dr. Jeffrey Seif, General Editor

A work from the moderate, conservative center of the Messianic Jewish revival. This book speaks to the interests that group and the Church have in Jews, Israel and eschatology, with a need for a more-balanced consideration of faith, theology and practice—from Jewish perspectives.

This is vital for the many tens of thousands of Jews who have come to faith and who participate in Messianic Jewish experience and also those who frequent churches. Our non-Jewish friends who associate with the Messianic Jewish movement will find this book beneficial as well. It represents some of our best thinking and practice. 314 pages

Paperback	978-1733935425	$26.99

The Lives and Ministries of ELIJAH and ELISHA
Demonstrating the Wonderful Power of the Word of God
—Dr. Walter C. Kaiser, Jr.

It's no wonder Old Testament professor Walt Kaiser is one of America's most beloved Bible expositors. This series of studies on Elijah and Elisha is vintage Kaiser, interspersed with his trademark humor. Organized in outline format, it offers an easy-to-follow look at the lives of two of the most famous and lively prophets ever to grace the pages of the Old Testament. Highly recommended to enhance anyone's study of the Scriptures! 182 pages

Paperback	978-1733935449	$17.99

Social Justice The Bible and Application for Our Times
—Daniel C. Juster

In this work, addressing many of the social justice issues of today, one of the more seasoned Messianic Jewish leaders and scholars, Dr. Dan Juster, offers his thoughts. Not an academic book, we read what this well-known pioneer of Messianic Judaism, director of Tikkun International, founding president of the Union of Messianic Jewish Congregations and senior pastor of Beth Messiah Congregation from 1978-2012, thinks about the way our world is today. You will find his thoughts challenging and surprising. 122 pages

Paperback	978-1733935456	$12.99

The Book of Ruth
This delightful version of *The Book of Ruth* includes the full text from the *Complete Jewish Bible* on the left page of the two-page spread. On the right are artful illustrations with brief story summaries that can be read to young children. Can be read any time during the year, but especially on *Shavuot* (Pentecost), the anniversary of the giving of the Torah on Mount Sinai and when the Holy Spirit was poured out on Yeshua's disciples (Acts 2). *The Book of Ruth* points to Yeshua as the ultimate Kinsman Redeemer.
6 x 9 inches, 26 pages with full color illustrations.

Paperback	978-1-936716-94-4	$ 9.99

The Book of Esther
This delightful version of *The Book of Esther* includes the full text from the *Complete Jewish Bible* on the left page of the two-page spread. On the right are artful illustrations with brief story summaries that can be read to young children. Can be read any time during the year, but especially during *Purim*, the festival that celebrates how Queen Esther risked her life and became a vessel for the deliverance of her people Israel. Though God is not mentioned, Mordecai and Esther humbled themselves before God by fasting and praying, which showed dependence upon him. God answered and delivered his people while bringing the proud Haman to justice.
6 x 9 inches, 34 pages with full color illustrations.

Paperback	978-1-936716-95-1	$ 9.99

Dear You
Letters of Identity in Yeshua ~ for Women ~
—Victoria Humphrey

Dear You is about discovering the truth of who you are as a beloved and courageous daughter of the King. It is an invitation to uncover what Elohim says about you through Scripture, silencing all other noise that vies to define you. While weaving together personal testimonies from other women, along with an opportunity to unearth your own unique story, it presents the challenge to leave a shallow life behind by taking a leap into the abundant life Yeshua offers. 232 Pages

| Paperback | 978-1-7339354-0-1 | $19.99 |

A Life of Favor
A Family Therapist Examines the Story of Joseph and His Brothers
—Rabbi Russell Resnik, MA, LPCC

Favor is an inherent part of God's reality as Father, and properly understood, is a source of blessing to those who want to know him. The story of Jacob's sons points to a life of favor that can make a difference in our lives today. Excellent insight—judgments in exegesis are matched by skillful use of counseling principles and creative applications to contemporary situations in life and in the family. —Walter C. Kaiser, Jr. President Emeritus, Gordon-Conwell Theological Seminary, Hamilton, Mass. 212 Pages

| Paperback | 978-1936716913 | $19.99 |

Will the Nazi Eagle Rise Again?
What the Church Needs to Know about BDS and Other Forces of Anti-Semitism
–David Friedman, Ph.D.

This is the right book at the right time. exposing the roots of Anti-Semitism being resurrected in our days, especially in our Christian Church.
—Dr. Hans-Jörg Kagi, Teacher, Theologian, Basle, Switzerland
Timely and important response to the dangerous hatred of the State of Israel that is growing in society and in the Church. 256 pages

| Paperback | 978-1936716876 | $19.99 |

The Day Jesus Did Tikkun Olam
—Richard A. Robinson, Ph.D.

Easy-to-read, yet scholarly, explores ancient Jewish and Christian scriptures, relevant stories and biblical parallels, to explain the most significant Jewish value—*tikkun olam*—making this world a better place. This is a tenet of both religions, central to the person of Jesus himself. 146 pages
—Murray Tilles, Director, Light of Messiah Ministries; M.Div.
A wealth of scholarship and contemporary relevance with great insight into Jewish ethics and the teachings of Jesus.
—Dr. Richard Harvey, Senior Researcher, Jews for Jesus

| Paperback | 978-1-936716-98-2 | $ 18.99 |

Jewish Giftedness & World Redemption
The Calling of Israel
—Jim Melnick

All things are mortal but the Jew; all other forces pass, but he remains. What is the secret of his immortality?

—Mark Twain, Concerning the Jews, *Harper's Magazine*, September, 1899.

The most comprehensive research of the unique achievements of the Jewish people. The author comes up with the only reason that makes sense of this mystery.

—Daniel C. Juster, Th.D., Restoration from Zion of Tikkun International

Paperback (280 Pages)   978-1-936716-88-3 $24.99

Messianic Judaism *A Modern Movement With an Ancient Past*
—David H. Stern

An updated discussion of the history, ideology, theology and program for Messianic Judaism. A challenge to both Jews and non-Jews who honor Yeshua to catch the vision of Messianic Judaism. 312 pages

Paperback   978-1880226339   **LB62** $17.99

Restoring the Jewishness of the Gospel
A Message for Christians
—David H. Stern

Introduces Christians to the Jewish roots of their faith, challenges some conventional ideas, and raises some neglected questions: How are both the Jews and "the Church" God's people? Is the Law of Moses in force today? Filled with insight! Endorsed by Dr. Darrell L. Bock. 110 pages

English - Paperback   978-1880226667   **LB70** $9.99
Spanish - Paperback   978-9653590175   **JB14** $9.99

The Return of the Kosher Pig *The Divine Messiah in Jewish Thought*
—Rabbi Tzahi Shapira

The subject of Messiah fills many pages of rabbinic writings. Hidden in those pages is a little known concept that the Messiah has the same authority given to God. Based on the Scriptures and traditional rabbinic writings, this book shows the deity of Yeshua from a new perspective. You will see that the rabbis of old expected the Messiah to be divine. Softcover, 352 pages.

"One of the most interesting and learned tomes I have ever read. Contained within its pages is much with which I agree, some with which I disagree, and much about which I never thought. Rabbi Shapria's remarkable book cannot be ignored."

—Dr. Paige Patterson, President, Southwest Baptist Theological Seminary

Paperback   978-1936716456   **LB81** $ 39.99

Messianic Jewish Commentary Series

Matthew Presents Yeshua, King Messiah
—Rabbi Barney Kasdan

Few commentators are able to truly present Yeshua in his Jewish context of his background, his family, even his religion. This commentator is well versed with first-century Jewish practices and thought, as well as the historical and cultural setting of the day, and the 'traditions of the Elders' that Yeshua so often spoke about. 448 pages

| Paperback | 978-1936716265 | **LB76** | $29.99 |

Rabbi Paul Enlightens the Ephesians on Walking with Messiah Yeshua
—Rabbi Barney Kasdan

The Ephesian were a diverse group of Jews and Gentiles, united together in Messiah. They definitely had an impact on the first century world in which they lived. But the Rabbi was not just writing to that local group. What is Paul saying to us? 160 pages.

| Paperback | 978-11936716821 | **LB99** | $17.99 |

Paul Presents to the Philippians Unity in the Messianic Community
—R. Sean Emslie

A worthy read and an appropriate study for any Messianic Jewish *talmid* or Christian disciple of Yeshua wanting to fairly and faithfully examine apostolic teaching. Emslie's investigation offers a keenly diligent analysis and faithfully responsible apostolic viewpoint. 165 pages

| Paperback | 978-1733935432 - Coming by June 30, 2020 | $18.99 |

James the Just Presents Application of Torah
—Dr. David Friedman

James (Jacob) one of the Epistles written to first century Jewish followers of Yeshua. Dr. David Friedman, a former Professor of the Israel Bible Institute has shed new light for Christians from this very important letter. 133 pages

| Paperback | 978-1936716449 | **LB82** | $14.99 |

John's Three Letters on Hope, Love and Covenant Fidelity
—Rabbi Joshua Brumbach

The Letters of John include some of the most beloved and often-quoted portions of scripture. Most people – scholars included – are confident they already have John's letters figured out. But do they really? There is a need for a fresh, post-supersessionist reading of John's letters that challenges common presuppositions regarding their purpose, message and relevance. 168 pages

| Paperback | 978-1-7339354-6-3 Coming by June 30, 2020 | $19.99 |

Jude On Faith and the Destructive Influence of Heresy
—Rabbi Joshua Brumbach

Almost no other canonical book has been as neglected and overlooked as the Epistle of Jude. This little book may be small, but it has a big message that is even more relevant today as when it was originally written. 100 pages

| Paperback | 978-1-936716-78-4 | **LB97** | $14.99 |

Yochanan (John) Presents the Revelation of Yeshua the Messiah
—Rabbi Gavriel Lumbroso

The Book of Revelation is perhaps the most mysterious, difficult-to-understand book in all of the Bible. Scholar after scholar, theologian after theologian have wrestled with all the strange visions, images and messages given by Yochanan (John), one of Yeshua's apostles. 206 pages

| Paperback | 978-1-936716-93-7 | $19.99 |

Psalms & Proverbs *Tehillim* תְהִלִּים-*Mishlei* מִשְׁלֵי
—Translated by Dr. David Stern

Contemplate the power in these words anytime, anywhere: Psalms-*Tehillim* offers uplifting words of praise and gratitude, keeping us focused with the right attitude; Proverbs-*Mishlei* gives us the wisdom for daily living, renewing our minds by leading us to examine our actions, to discern good from evil, and to decide freely to do the good. Makes a wonderful and meaningful gift. 224 pages.

| Paperback | 978-1936716692 | **LB90** | $9.99 |

At the Feet of Rabbi Gamaliel
Rabbinic Influence in Paul's Teachings
—David Friedman, Ph.D.

Paul (Shaul) was on the "fast track" to becoming a sage and Sanhedrin judge, describing himself as passionate for the Torah and the traditions of the fathers, typical for an aspiring Pharisee: "...trained at the feet of Gamaliel in every detail of the Torah of our forefathers. I was a zealot for God, as all of you are today" (Acts 22.3, CJB). Did Shaul's teachings reflect Rabbi Gamaliel's instructions? Did Paul continue to value the Torah and Pharisaic tradition? Did Paul create a 'New' Theology? The results of the research within these pages and its conclusion may surprise you. 100 pages.

| Paperback | 978-1936716753 | **LB95** | $8.99 |

Debranding God *Revealing His True Essence*
—Eduardo Stein

The process of 'debranding' God is to remove all the labels and fads that prompt us to understand him as a supplier and ourselves as the most demanding of customers. Changing our perception of God also changes our perception of ourselves. In knowing who we are in relationship to God, we discover his, and our, true essence. 252 pages.

| Paperback | 978-1936716708 | **LB91** | $16.99 |

Under the Fig Tree *Messianic Thought Through the Hebrew Calendar*
—Patrick Gabriel Lumbroso

Take a daily devotional journey into the Word of God through the Hebrew Calendar and the Biblical Feasts. Learn deeper meaning of the Scriptures through Hebraic thought. Beautifully written and a source for inspiration to draw closer to Adonai every day. 407 pages.

| Paperback | 978-1936716760 | **LB96** | $25.99 |

Under the Vine *Messianic Thought Through the Hebrew Calendar*
—Patrick Gabriel Lumbroso

Journey daily through the Hebrew Calendar and Biblical Feasts into the B'rit Hadashah (New Testament) Scriptures as they are put in their rightful context, bringing Judaism alive in it's full beauty. Messianic faith was the motor and what gave substance to Abraham's new beliefs, hope to Job, trust to Isaac, vision to Jacob, resilience to Joseph, courage to David, wisdom to Solomon, knowledge to Daniel, and divine Messianic authority to Yeshua. 412 pages.

| Paperback | 978-1936716654 | **LB87** | $25.99 |

Come and Worship *Ways to Worship from the Hebrew Scriptures*
—Compiled by Barbara D. Malda

We were created to worship. God has graciously given us many ways to express our praise to him. Each way fits a different situation or moment in life, yet all are intended to bring honor and glory to him. When we believe that he is who he says he is [see *His Names are Wonderful!*] and that his Word is true, worship flows naturally from our hearts to his. 128 pages.

Paperback	978-1936716678	**LB88**	$9.99

His Names Are Wonderful
Getting to Know God Through His Hebrew Names
—Elizabeth L. Vander Meulen and Barbara D. Malda

In Hebrew thought, names did more than identify people; they revealed their nature. God's identity is expressed not in one name, but in many. This book will help readers know God better as they uncover the truths in his Hebrew names. 160 pages.

Paperback	978-1880226308	**LB58**	$9.99

The Revolt of Rabbi Morris Cohen
Exploring the Passion & Piety of a Modern-day Pharisee
—Anthony Cardinale

A brilliant school psychologist, Rabbi Morris Cohen went on a one-man strike to protest the systematic mislabeling of slow learning pupils as "Learning Disabled" (to extract special education money from the state). His disciplinary hearing, based on the transcript, is a hilarious read! This effusive, garrulous man with an irresistible sense of humor lost his job, but achieved a major historic victory causing the reform of the billion-dollar special education program. Enter into the mind of an eighth-generation Orthodox rabbi to see how he deals spiritually with the loss of everything, even the love of his children. This modern-day Pharisee discovered a trusted friend in the author (a born again believer in Jesus) with whom he could openly struggle over Rabbinic Judaism as well as the concept of Jesus (Yeshua) as Messiah. 320 pages.

Paperback	978-1936716722	**LB92**	$19.99

Stories of Yeshua
—Jim Reimann, Illustrator Julia Filipone-Erez

Children's Bible Storybook with four stories about Yeshua (Jesus).
Yeshua is Born: The Bethlehem Story based on Lk 1:26-35 & 2:1-20; *Yeshua and Nicodemus in Jerusalem* based on Jn 3:1-16; *Yeshua Loves the Little Children of the World* based on Matthew 18:1–6 & 19:13–15; *Yeshua is Alive-The Empty Tomb in Jerusalem* based on Matthew 26:17-56, Jn 19:16-20:18, Lk 24:50-53. Ages 3-7, 48 pages.

Paperback	978-1936716685	**LB89**	$14.99

To the Ends of the Earth – How the First Jewish Followers of Yeshua Transformed the Ancient World
— Dr. Jeffrey Seif

Everyone knows that the first followers of Yeshua were Jews, and that Christianity was very Jewish for the first 50 to 100 years. It's a known fact that there were many congregations made up mostly of Jews, although the false perception today is, that in the second century they disappeared. Dr. Seif reveals the truth of what happened to them and how these early Messianic Jews influenced and transformed the behavior of the known world at that time. 171 pages

Paperback	978-1936716463	**LB83**	$17.99

Jewish Roots and Foundations of the Scriptures I & II
—John Fischer, Th.D, Ph.D.

An outstanding evangelical leader once said: "There is something shallow about a Christianity that has lost its Jewish roots." A beautiful painting is a careful interweaving of a number of elements. Among other things, there are the background, the foreground and the subject. Discovering the roots of your faith is a little like appreciating the various parts of a painting. In the background is the panorama of preparation and pictures found in the Old Testament. In the foreground is the landscape and light of the first century Jewish setting. All of this is intricately connected with and highlights the subject—which becomes the flowering of all these aspects—the coming of God to earth and what that means for us. Discovering and appreciating your roots in this way broadens, deepens and enriches your faith and your understanding of Scripture. This audio is 32 hours of live class instruction - audio is clear and easy to understand.

9781936716623   **LCD03 / LCD04** $49.99 each

The Gospels in their Jewish Context
—John Fischer, Th.D, Ph.D.

An examination of the Jewish background and nature of the Gospels in their contemporary political, cultural and historical settings, emphasizing each gospel's special literary presentation of Yeshua, and highlighting the cultural and religious contexts necessary for understanding each of the gospels. 32 hours of audio/video instruction on MP3-DVD and pdf of syllabus.

978-1936716241   **LCD01** $49.99

The Epistles from a Jewish Perspective
—John Fischer, Th.D, Ph.D.

An examination of the relationship of Rabbi Shaul (the Apostle Paul) and the Apostles to their Jewish contemporaries and environment; surveys their Jewish practices, teaching, controversy with the religious leaders, and many critical passages, with emphasis on the Jewish nature, content, and background of these letters. 32 hours of audio/video instruction on MP3-DVD and pdf of syllabus.

978-1936716258   **LCD02** $49.99

The Red Heifer *A Jewish Cry for Messiah*
—Anthony Cardinale

Award-winning journalist and playwright Anthony Cardinale has traveled extensively in Israel, and recounts here his interviews with Orthodox rabbis, secular Israelis, and Palestinian Arabs about the current search for a red heifer by Jewish radicals wishing to rebuild the Temple and bring the Messiah. These real-life interviews are interwoven within an engaging and dramatic fictional portrayal of the diverse people of Israel and how they would react should that red heifer be found. Readers will find themselves in the Land, where they can hear learned rabbis and ordinary Israelis talking about the red heifer and dealing with all the related issues and the imminent coming and identity of Messiah. 341 pages

Paperback   978-1936716470   **LB79** $19.99

The Borough Park Papers
—Multiple Authors

As you read the New Testament, you "overhear" debates first-century Messianic Jews had about critical issues, e.g. Gentiles being "allowed" into the Messianic kingdom (Acts 15). Similarly, you're now invited to "listen in" as leading twenty-first century Messianic Jewish theologians discuss critical issues facing us today. Some ideas may not fit into your previously held pre-suppositions or pre-conceptions. Indeed, you may find some paradigm shifting in your thinking. We want to share the thoughts of these thinkers with you, our family in the Messiah.

Symposium I:
The Gospel and the Jewish People
248 pages, Paperback   978-1936716593   **LB84** $39.95

Symposium II:
The Deity of Messiah and the Mystery of God
211 pages, Paperback   978-1936716609   **LB85** $39.95

Symposium III:
How Jewish Should the Messianic Community Be?
Paperback   978-1936716616   **LB86** $39.95

Passion for Israel: *A Short History of the Evangelical Church's Support of Israel and the Jewish People*
—Dan Juster

History reveals a special commitment of Christians to the Jews as God's still elect people, but the terrible atrocities committed against the Jews by so-called Christians have overshadowed the many good deeds that have been performed. This important history needs to be told to help heal the wounds and to inspire more Christians to stand together in support of Israel. 84 pages

Paperback   978-1936716401   **LB78** $9.99

On The Way to Emmaus: *Searching the Messianic Prophecies*
—Dr. Jacques Doukhan

An outstanding compilation of the most critical Messianic prophecies by a renowned conservative Christian Scholar, drawing on material from the Bible, Rabbinic sources, Dead Sea Scrolls, and more. 217 pages

Paperback   978-1936716432   **LB80** $14.99

Yeshua *A Guide to the Real Jesus and the Original Church*
—Dr. Ron Moseley

Opens up the history of the Jewish roots of the Christian faith. Illuminates the Jewish background of Yeshua and the Church and never flinches from showing "Jesus was a Jew, who was born, lived, and died, within first century Judaism." Explains idioms in the New Testament. Endorsed by Dr. Brad Young and Dr. Marvin Wilson. 213 pages.

Paperback   978-1880226681   **LB29** $12.99

Gateways to Torah *Joining the Ancient Conversation on the Weekly Portion*
—Rabbi Russell Resnik

From before the days of Messiah until today, Jewish people have read from and discussed a prescribed portion of the Pentateuch each week. Now, a Messianic Jewish Rabbi, Russell Resnik, brings another perspective on the Torah, that of a Messianic Jew. 246 pages.

Paperback	978-1880226889	**LB42**	$15.99

Creation to Completion *A Guide to Life's Journey from the Five Books of Moses*
—Rabbi Russell Resnik

Endorsed by Coach Bill McCartney, Founder of Promise Keepers & Road to Jerusalem: "Paul urged Timothy to study the Scriptures (2 Tim. 3:16), advising him to apply its teachings to all aspects of his life. Since there was no New Testament then, this rabbi/apostle was convinced that his disciple would profit from studying the Torah, the Five Books of Moses, and the Old Testament. Now, Rabbi Resnik has written a warm devotional commentary that will help you understand and apply the Law of Moses to your life in a practical way." 256 pages

Paperback	978-1880226322	**LB61**	$14.99

Walk Genesis! Walk Exodus! Walk Leviticus! Walk Numbers! Walk Deuteronomy!
Messianic Jewish Devotional Commentaries
—Jeffrey Enoch Feinberg, Ph.D.

Using the weekly synagogue readings, Dr. Jeffrey Feinberg has put together some very valuable material in his "Walk" series. Each section includes a short Hebrew lesson (for the non-Hebrew speaker), key concepts, an excellent overview of the portion, and some practical applications. Can be used as a daily devotional as well as a Bible study tool.Paperback.

Walk Genesis!	238 pages	978-1880226759	**LB34**	$12.99
Walk Exodus!	224 pages	978-1880226872	**LB40**	$12.99
Walk Leviticus!	208 pages	978-1880226926	**LB45**	$12.99
Walk Numbers!	211 pages	978-1880226995	**LB48**	$12.99
Walk Deuteronomy!	231 pages	978-1880226186	**LB51**	$12.99
SPECIAL! Five-book Walk!		5 Book Set **Save $10**	**LK28**	$54.99

Good News According To Matthew

—Dr. Henry Einspruch

English translation with quotations from the Tanakh (Old Testament) capitalized and printed in Hebrew. Helpful notations are included. Lovely black and white illustrations throughout the book. 86 pages.

Paperback	978-1880226025	**LB03**	$4.99
Also available in Yiddish.		**LB02**	$4.99

They Loved the Torah *What Yeshua's First Followers Really Thought About the Law*

—Dr. David Friedman

Although many Jews believe that Paul taught against the Law, this book disproves that notion. An excellent case for his premise that all the first followers of the Messiah were not only Torah-observant, but also desired to spread their love for God's entire Word to the gentiles to whom they preached. 144 pages. Endorsed by Dr. David Stern, Ariel Berkowitz, Rabbi Dr. Stuart Dauermann & Dr. John Fischer.

Paperback	978-1880226940	**LB47**	$9.99

The Distortion *2000 Years of Misrepresenting the Relationship Between Jesus the Messiah and the Jewish People*

—Dr. John Fischer & Dr. Patrice Fischer

Did the Jews kill Jesus? Did they really reject him? With the rise of global anti–Semitism, it is important to understand what the Gospels teach about the relationship between Jewish people and their Messiah. 2000 years of distortion have made this difficult. Learn how the distortion began and continues to this day and what you can do to change it. 126 pages. Endorsed by Dr. Ruth Fleischer, Rabbi Russell Resnik, Dr. Daniel C. Juster, Dr. Michael Rydelnik.

Paperback	978-1880226254	**LB54**	$11.99

---

eBooks Now Available!

Versions available for your favorite reader

Visit www.messianicjewish.net for direct links to these readers for each available eBook.

God's Appointed Times *A Practical Guide to Understanding and Celebrating the Biblical Holidays* – **New Edition.**
—Rabbi Barney Kasdan

The Biblical Holy Days teach us about the nature of God and his plan for mankind, and can be a source of God's blessing for all believers–Jews and Gentiles–today. Includes historical background, traditional Jewish observance, New Testament relevance, and prophetic significance, plus music, crafts and holiday recipes. 145 pages.

English - Paperback	978-1880226353	**LB63**	$12.99
Spanish - Paperback	978-1880226391	**LB59**	$12.99

God's Appointed Customs *A Messianic Jewish Guide to the Biblical Lifecycle and Lifestyle*
— Rabbi Barney Kasdan

Explains how biblical customs are often the missing key to unlocking the depths of Scripture. Discusses circumcision, the Jewish wedding, and many more customs mentioned in the New Testament. Companion to *God's Appointed Times*. 170 pages.

English - Paperback	978-1880226636	**LB26**	$12.99
Spanish - Paperback	978-1880226551	**LB60**	$12.99

Celebrations of the Bible *A Messianic Children's Curriculum*

Did you know that each Old Testament feast or festival finds its fulfillment in the New? They enrich the lives of people who experience and enjoy them. Our popular curriculum for children is in a brand new, user-friendly format. The lay-flat at binding allows you to easily reproduce handouts and worksheets. Celebrations of the Bible has been used by congregations, Sunday schools, ministries, homeschoolers, and individuals to teach children about the biblical festivals. Each of these holidays are presented for Preschool (2-K), Primary (Grades 1-3), Junior (Grades 4-6), and Children's Worship/Special Services. 208 pages.

Paperback	978-1880226261	**LB55**	$24.99

Passover: *The Key That Unlocks the Book of Revelation*
—Daniel C. Juster, Th.D.

Is there any more enigmatic book of the Bible than Revelation? Controversy concerning its meaning has surrounded it back to the first century. Today, the arguments continue. Yet, Dan Juster has given us the key that unlocks the entire book—the events and circumstances of the Passover/Exodus. By interpreting Revelation through the lens of Exodus, Dan Juster provides a unified overview that helps us read Revelation as it was always meant to be read, as a drama of spiritual conflict, deliverance, and above all, worship. He also shows how this final drama, fulfilled in Messiah, resonates with the Torah and all of God's Word. — Russ Resnik, Executive Director, Union of Messianic Jewish Congregations.

Paperback	978-1936716210	**LB74**	$10.99

The Messianic Passover Haggadah
Revised and Updated
—Rabbi Barry Rubin and Steffi Rubin.

Guides you through the traditional Passover seder dinner, step-by-step. Not only does this observance remind us of our rescue from Egyptian bondage, but, we remember Messiah's last supper, a Passover seder. The theme of redemption is seen throughout the evening. What's so unique about our Haggadah is the focus on Yeshua (Jesus) the Messiah and his teaching, especially on his last night in the upper room. 36 pages.

English - Paperback	978-1880226292	**LB57**	$4.99
Spanish - Paperback	978-1880226599	**LBSP01**	$4.99

The Messianic Passover Seder Preparation Guide
Includes recipes, blessings and songs. 19 pages.

English - Paperback	978-1880226247	**LB10**	$2.99
Spanish - Paperback	978-1880226728	**LBSP02**	$2.99

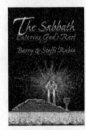

The Sabbath *Entering God's Rest*
—Barry Rubin & Steffi Rubin

Even if you've never celebrated Shabbat before, this book will guide you into the rest God has for all who would enter in—Jews and non-Jews. Contains prayers, music, recipes; in short, everything you need to enjoy the Sabbath, even how to observe havdalah, the closing ceremony of the Sabbath. Also discusses the Saturday or Sunday controversy. 48 pages.

Paperback	978-1880226742	**LB32**	$6.99

Havdalah *The Ceremony that Completes the Sabbath*
—Dr. Neal & Jamie Lash

The Sabbath ends with this short, yet equally sweet ceremony called havdalah (separation). This ceremony reminds us to be a light and a sweet fragrance in this world of darkness as we carry the peace, rest, joy and love of the Sabbath into the work week. 28 pages.

Paperback	978-1880226605	**LB69**	$4.99

Dedicate and Celebrate!
A Messianic Jewish Guide to Hanukkah
—Barry Rubin & Family

Hanukkah means "dedication" — a theme of significance for Jews and Christians. Discussing its historical background, its modern-day customs, deep meaning for all of God's people, this little book covers all the how-tos! Recipes, music, and prayers for lighting the menorah, all included! 32 pages.

Paperback	978-1880226834	**LB36**	$4.99

The Conversation
An Intimate Journal of the Emmaus Encounter
—Judy Salisbury

"Then beginning with Moses and with all the prophets, He explained to them the things concerning Himself in all the Scriptures." Luke 24:27

If you've ever wondered what that conversation must have been like, this captivating book takes you there.

"The Conversation brings to life that famous encounter between the two disciples and our Lord Jesus on the road to Emmaus. While it is based in part on an imaginative reconstruction, it is filled with the throbbing pulse of the excitement of the sensational impact that our Lord's resurrection should have on all of our lives." ~ Dr. Walter Kaiser President Emeritus Gordon-Conwell Theological Seminary. Hardcover 120 pages.

Hardcover	978-1936716173	**LB73**	$14.99
Paperback	978-1936716364	**LB77**	$9.99

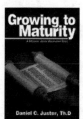

Growing to Maturity
A Messianic Jewish Discipleship Guide
—Daniel C. Juster, Th.D.

This discipleship series presents first steps of understanding and spiritual practice, tailored for the Jewish believer. It's purpose is to aid the believer in living according to Yeshua's will as a disciple, one who has learned the example of his teacher. The course is structured according to recent advances in individualized educational instruction. Discipleship is serious business and the material is geared for serious study and reflection. Each chapter is divided into short sections followed by study questions. 256 pages.

Paperback	978-1936716227	**LB75**	$19.99

Growing to Maturity Primer: *A Messianic Jewish Discipleship Workbook*
—Daniel C. Juster, Th.D.

A basic book of material in question and answer form. Usable by everyone. 60 pages.

Paperback	978-0961455507	**TB16**	$7.99

Conveying Our Heritage A Messianic Jewish Guide to Home Practice
—Daniel C. Juster, Th.D. Patricia A. Juster

Throughout history the heritage of faith has been conveyed within the family and the congregation. The first institution in the Bible is the family and only the family can raise children with an adequate appreciation of our faith and heritage. This guide exists to help families learn how to pass on the heritage of spiritual Messianic Jewish life. Softcover, 86 pages

Paperback	978-1936716739	**LB93**	$8.99

That They May Be One *A Brief Review of Church Restoration Movements and Their Connection to the Jewish People*
—Daniel Juster, Th.D

Something prophetic and momentous is happening. The Church is finally fully grasping its relationship to Israel and the Jewish people. Author describes the restoration movements in Church history and how they connected to Israel and the Jewish people. Each one contributed in some way—some more, some less—toward the ultimate unity between Jews and Gentiles. Predicted in the Old Testament and fulfilled in the New, Juster believes this plan of God finds its full expression in Messianic Judaism. He may be right. See what you think as you read *That They May Be One*. 100 pages.

Paperback	978-1880226711	**LB71**	$9.99

The Greatest Commandment
How the Sh'ma Leads to More Love in Your Life
—Irene Lipson

"What is the greatest commandment?" Yeshua was asked. His reply—"Hear, O Israel, the Lord our God, the Lord is one, and you are to love Adonai your God with all your heart, with all your soul, with all your understanding, and all your strength." A superb book explaining each word so the meaning can be fully grasped and lived. Endorsed by Elliot Klayman, Susan Perlman, & Robert Stearns. 175 pages.

Paperback	978-1880226360	**LB65**	$12.99

Blessing the King of the Universe
Transforming Your Life Through the Practice of Biblical Praise
—Irene Lipson

Insights into the ancient biblical practice of blessing God are offered clearly and practically. With examples from Scripture and Jewish tradition, this book teaches the biblical formula used by men and women of the Bible, including the Messiah; points to new ways and reasons to praise the Lord; and explains more about the Jewish roots of the faith. Endorsed by Rabbi Barney Kasdan, Dr. Mitch Glaser, & Rabbi Dr. Dan Cohn-Sherbok. 144 pages.

Paperback	978-1880226797	**LB53**	$11.99

You Bring the Bagels, I'll Bring the Gospel
Sharing the Messiah with Your Jewish Neighbor
Revised Edition—Now with Study Questions
—Rabbi Barry Rubin

This "how-to-witness-to-Jewish-people" book is an orderly presentation of everything you need to share the Messiah with a Jewish friend. Includes Messianic prophecies, Jewish objections to believing, sensitivities in your witness, words to avoid. A "must read" for all who care about the Jewish people. Good for individual or group study. Used in Bible schools. Endorsed by Harold A. Sevener, Dr. Walter C. Kaiser, Dr. Erwin J. Kolb and Dr. Arthur F. Glasser. 253 pages, Paperback.

English	978-1880226650	**LB13**	$12.99
Te Tengo Buenas Noticias	978-0829724103	**OBSP02**	$14.99

Making Eye Contact With God
A Weekly Devotional for Women
—Terri Gillespie

What kind of eyes do you have? Are they downcast and sad? Are they full of God's joy and passion? See yourself through the eyes of God. Using real life anecdotes, combined with scripture, the author reveals God's heart for women everywhere, as she softly speaks of the ways in which women see God. Endorsed by prominent authors: Dr. Angela Hunt, Wanda Dyson and Kathryn Mackel. 247 pages.

| Hardcover | 978-1880226513 | **LB68** | $19.99 |

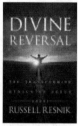

Divine Reversal
The Transforming Ethics of Jesus
—Rabbi Russell Resnik

In the Old Testament, God often reversed the plans of man. Yeshua's ethics continue this theme. Following his path transforms one's life from within, revealing the source of true happiness, forgiveness, reconciliation, fidelity and love. From the introduction, "As a Jewish teacher, Jesus doesn't separate matters of theology from practice. His teaching is consistently practical, ethical, and applicable to real life, even two thousand years after it was originally given." Endorsed by Jonathan Bernis, Dr. Daniel C. Juster, Dr. Jeffrey L. Seif, and Dr Darrell Bock. 206 pages

| Paperback | 978-1880226803 | **LB72** | $12.99 |

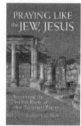

Praying Like the Jew, Jesus
Recovering the Ancient Roots of New Testament Prayer
—Dr. Timothy P. Jones

This eye-opening book reveals the Jewish background of many of Yeshua's prayers. Historical vignettes "transport" you to the times of Yeshua so you can grasp the full meaning of Messiah's prayers. Unique devotional thoughts and meditations, presented in down-to-earth language, provide inspiration for a more meaningful prayer life and help you draw closer to God. Endorsed by Mark Galli, James W. Goll, Rev. Robert Stearns, James F. Strange, and Dr. John Fischer. 144 pages.

| Paperback | 978-1880226285 | **LB56** | $9.99 |

Growing Your Olive Tree Marriage *A Guide for Couples from Two Traditions*
—David J. Rudolph

One partner is Jewish; the other is Christian. Do they celebrate Hanukkah, Christmas or both? Do they worship in a church or a synagogue? How will the children be raised? This is the first book from a biblical perspective that addresses the concerns of intermarried couples, offering a godly solution. Includes highlights of interviews with intermarried couples. Endorsed by Walter C. Kaiser, Jr., Rabbi Dan Cohn-Sherbok, Jonathan Settel, Dr. Mitchell Glaser & Natalie Sirota. 224 pages.

| Paperback | 978-1880226179 | **LB50** | $12.99 |

In Search of the Silver Lining *Where is God in the Midst of Life's Storms?*
—Jerry Gramckow

When faced with suffering, what are your choices? Storms have always raged. And people have either perished in their wake or risen above the tempests, shaping history by their responses…new storms are on the horizon. How will we deal with them? How will we shape history or those who follow us? The answer lies in how we view God in the midst of the storms. Endorsed by Joseph C. Aldrich, Ray Beeson, Dr. Daniel Juster. 176 pages.

Paperback	978-1880226865	**LB39**	$10.99

The Voice of the Lord *Messianic Jewish Daily Devotional*
—Edited by David J. Rudolph

Brings insight into the Jewish Scriptures—both Old and New Testaments. Twenty-two prominent Messianic contributors provide practical ways to apply biblical truth. Start your day with this unique resource. Explanatory notes. Perfect companion to the Complete Jewish Bible (see page 2). Endorsed by Edith Schaeffer, Dr. Arthur F. Glaser, Dr. Michael L. Brown, Mitch Glaser and Moishe Rosen. 416 pages.

Paperback	9781880226704	**LB31**	$19.99

Kingdom Relationships *God's Laws for the Community of Faith*
—Dr. Ron Moseley

Dr. Ron Moseley`s Yeshua: A Guide to the Real Jesus and the Original Church has taught thousands of people about the Jewishness of not only Yeshua, but of the first followers of the Messiah.

In this work, Moseley focuses on the teaching of Torah -- the Five Books of Moses -- tapping into truths that greatly help modern-day members of the community of faith. 64 pages.

Paperback	978-1880226841	**LB37**	$8.99

Mutual Blessing *Discovering the Ultimate Destiny of Creation*
—Daniel C. Juster

To truly love as God loves is to see the wonder and richness of the distinct differences in all of creation and his natural order of interdependence. This is the way to mutual blessing and the discovery of the ultimate destiny of creation. Learn how to become enriched and blessed as you enrich and bless others and all that is around you! Softcover, 135 pages.

Paperback	978-1936716746	**LB94**	$9.99

Train Up A Child *Successful Parenting For The Next Generation*
—Dr. Daniel L. Switzer

The author, former principal of Ets Chaiyim Messianic Jewish Day School, and father of four, combines solid biblical teaching with Jewish sources on child raising, focusing on the biblical holy days, giving fresh insight into fulfilling the role of parent. 188 pages. Endorsed by Dr. David J. Rudolph, Paul Lieberman, and Dr. David H. Stern.

Paperback	978-1880226377	**LB64**	$12.99

Fire on the Mountain - *Past Renewals, Present Revivals and the Coming Return of Israel*
—Dr. Louis Goldberg

The term "revival" is often used to describe a person or congregation turning to God. Is this something that "just happens," or can it be brought about? Dr. Louis Goldberg, author and former professor of Hebrew and Jewish Studies at Moody Bible Institute, examines real revivals that took place in Bible times and applies them to today. 268 pages.

| Paperback | 978-1880226858 | **LB38** | $15.99 |

Voices of Messianic Judaism *Confronting Critical Issues Facing a Maturing Movement*
—General Editor Rabbi Dan Cohn-Sherbok

Many of the best minds of the Messianic Jewish movement contributed their thoughts to this collection of 29 substantive articles. Challenging questions are debated: The involvement of Gentiles in Messianic Judaism? How should outreach be accomplished? Liturgy or not? Intermarriage? 256 pages.

| Paperback | 978-1880226933 | **LB46** | $15.99 |

The Enduring Paradox *Exploratory Essays in Messianic Judaism*
—General Editor Dr. John Fischer

Yeshua and his Jewish followers began a new movement—Messianic Judaism—2,000 years ago. In the 20th century, it was reborn. Now, at the beginning of the 21st century, it is maturing. Twelve essays from top contributors to the theology of this vital movement of God, including: Dr. Walter C. Kaiser, Dr. David H. Stern, and Dr. John Fischer. 196 pages.

| Paperback | 978-1880226902 | **LB43** | $13.99 |

The World To Come *A Portal to Heaven on Earth*
—Derek Leman

An insightful book, exposing fallacies and false teachings surrounding this extremely important subject... paints a hopeful picture of the future and dispels many non-biblical notions. Intriguing chapters: Magic and Desire, The Vision of the Prophets, Hints of Heaven, Horrors of Hell, The Drama of the Coming Ages. Offers a fresh, but old, perspective on the world to come, as it interacts with the prophets of Israel and the Bible. 110 pages.

| Paperback | 978-1880226049 | **LB67** | $9.99 |

Hebrews Through a Hebrew's Eyes
—Dr. Stuart Sacks

Written to first-century Messianic Jews, this epistle, understood through Jewish eyes, edifies and encourages all. 119 pages. Endorsed by Dr. R.C. Sproul and James M. Boice.

| Paperback | 978-1880226612 | **LB23** | $10.99 |

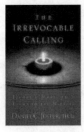

The Irrevocable Calling *Israel's Role As A Light To The Nations*
—Daniel C. Juster, Th.D.

Referring to the chosen-ness of the Jewish people, Paul, the Apostle, wrote "For God's free gifts and his calling are irrevocable" (Rom. 11:29). This messenger to the Gentiles understood the unique calling of his people, Israel. So does Dr. Daniel Juster, President of Tikkun Ministries Int'l. In *The Irrevocable Calling*, he expands Paul's words, showing how Israel was uniquely chosen to bless the world and how these blessings can be enjoyed today. Endorsed by Dr. Jack Hayford, Mike Bickle and Don Finto. 64 pages.

Paperback	978-1880226346	**LB66**	$8.99

Are There Two Ways of Atonement?
—Dr. Louis Goldberg

Here Dr. Louis Goldberg, long-time professor of Jewish Studies at Moody Bible Institute, exposes the dangerous doctrine of Two-Covenant Theology. 32 pages.

Paperback	978-1880226056	**LB12**	$ 4.99

Awakening *Articles and Stories About Jews and Yeshua*
—Arranged by Anna Portnov

Articles, testimonies, and stories about Jewish people and their relationship with God, Israel, and the Messiah. Includes the effective tract, "The Most Famous Jew of All." One of our best anthologies for witnessing to Jewish people. Let this book witness for you! Russian version also available. 110 pages.

English - Paperback	978-1880226094	**LB15**	$ 6.99
Russian - Paperback	978-1880226018	**LB14**	$ 6.99

The Unpromised Land *The Struggle of Messianic Jews Gary and Shirley Beresford*
—Linda Alexander

They felt God calling them to live in Israel, the Promised Land. Wanting nothing more than to live quietly and grow old together in the country of refuge for all Jewish people, little did they suspect what events would follow to try their faith. The fight to make *aliyah*, to claim their rightful inheritance in the Promised Land, became a battle waged not only for themselves, but also for Messianic Jews all over the world that wish to return to the Jewish homeland. Here is the true saga of the Beresford's journey to the land of their forefathers. 216 pages.

Paperback	978-1880226568	**LB19**	$ 9.99

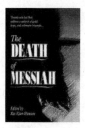

Death of Messiah *Twenty fascinating articles that address a subject of grief, hope, and ultimate triumph.*
—Edited by Kai Kjaer-Hansen

This compilation, written by well-known Jewish believers, addresses the issue of Messiah and offers proof that Yeshua—the true Messiah—not only died, but also was resurrected! 160 pages.

Paperback	978-1880226582	**LB20**	$ 8.99

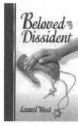

Beloved Dissident *(A Novel)*
—Laurel West

A gripping story of human relationships, passionate love, faith, and spiritual testing. Set in the world of high finance, intrigue, and international terrorism, the lives of David, Jonathan, and Leah intermingle on many levels--especially their relationships with one another and with God. As the two men tangle with each other in a rising whirlwind of excitement and danger, each hopes to win the fight for Leah's love. One of these rivals will move Leah to a level of commitment and love she has never imagined--or dared to dream. Whom will she choose? 256 pages.

Paperback	978-1880226766	**LB33**	$ 9.99

Sudden Terror
—Dr. David Friedman

Exposes the hidden agenda of militant Islam. The author, a former member of the Israel Defense Forces, provides eye-opening information needed in today's dangerous world.

Dr. David Friedman recounts his experiences confronting terrorism; analyzes the biblical roots of the conflict between Israel and Islam; provides an overview of early Islam; demonstrates how the United States and Israel are bound together by a common enemy; and shows how to cope with terrorism and conquer fear. The culmination of many years of research and personal experiences. This expose will prepare you for what's to come! 160 pages.

Paperback	978-1880226155	**LB49**	$ 9.99

It is Good! *Growing Up in a Messianic Family*
—Steffi Rubin

Growing up in a Messianic Jewish family. Meet Tovah! Tovah (Hebrew for "Good") is growing up in a Messianic Jewish home, learning the meaning of God's special days. Ideal for young children, it teaches the biblical holidays and celebrates faith in Yeshua. 32 pages to read & color.

Paperback	978-1880226063	**LB11**	$ 4.99